D1067659

OFFICIALLY WITHDRAWN
NEW HAVEN FREE PUBLIC LIBRARY

STETSON BRANCH
200 DIXWELL AVENUE
NEW HAVEN, CT 06511

DATE DUE

NEW HAVEN FREE PUBLIC LIBRARY
133 ELM STREET
NEW HAVEN, CT 06510

AVISSON YOUNG ADULT SERIES

BLACKBALL SUPERSTARS:
Legendary Players
of the
Negro Baseball Leagues

Ace Collins
and
John Hillman

Avisson Press, Inc.
Greensboro

Copyright © 1999 by Ace Collins and John Hillman. All rights reserved. For information, contact Avisson Press Inc., P.O. Box 38816, Greensboro, North Carolina 27438 USA.

First edition
Printed in the United States of America
ISBN 1-888105-38-0

Library of Congress Cataloging-in-Publication Data

Collins, Ace.
   Blackball superstars : legendary players of the Negro baseball leagues / Ace Collins and John Hillman. —1st ed.
      p.   cm. — (Avisson young adult series)
   Includes bibliographical references and index.
   Summary: Profiles twelve baseball players who labored in the Negro leagues formed near the turn of the century because African Americans were not allowed in the major leagues from 1898 until 1947.
   ISBN 1-888105-38-0 (lib. bdg.)
   1. Afro-American baseball players Biography Juvenile literature. 2. Negro leagues Juvenile literature. 3. Baseball—United States—History Juvenile literature [1. Negro leagues. 2. Afro-Americans Biography. 3. Baseball players. 4. Baseball—History.] I. Hillman, John. II. Title. III. Series.
GV865.A1C593   1999
796.357'089'96073—dc21   99-19370
                                                              CIP

PHOTO CREDITS: all photographs courtesy of the Negro Leagues Baseball Museum, Inc.

Stetson Branch Library
200 Dixwell Avenue
New Haven, CT 06511

796.357
COLLINS

Contents

INTRODUCTION 5

LEROY "SATCHEL" PAIGE 13

JOSHUA "JOSH" GIBSON 29

WALTER "BUCK" LEONARD 41

JAMES "COOL PAPA" BELL 51

WILLIAM "JUDY" JOHNSON 61

OSCAR CHARLESTON 71

JOHN HENRY "POP" LLOYD 79

ANDREW "RUBE" FOSTER 89

RAY "DANDY" DANDRIDGE 101

LEON DAY 109

WILLIE "BILL" FOSTER 119

WILLIE "THE DEVIL" WELLS 127

BIBLIOGRAPHY 135

INDEX 139

Introduction

They stood in the shadows of baseball, looking out. They came from Texas, Mississippi, Indiana, North Carolina, Georgia, Virginia, and Delaware to play in the industrial cities of the East and Midwest. They endured long days, poor food, substandard lodging, and sometimes-blatant bigotry. Yet they relished every moment in the sun or under the lights. These were the talented athletes of the Negro Leagues, pushed to less-glorious fields and stadiums than those of their white colleagues of the larger and more famous Major Leagues, the so-called "big leagues" of baseball.

Blackball Superstars reveals the tragedies and triumphs of a dozen men who played in and were stars of these same Negro Leagues. And very great players they were, so good that, finally and retroactively, they were inducted into the National Baseball Hall of Fame and Museum in Cooperstown, New York, generally known as the Hall of Fame. This is the highest honor that organized baseball can bestow on a player, living or dead.

Except for Leroy "Satchel" Paige (who played well into middle age), the athletes in the following pages never played for major league teams such as the Yankees, Dodgers, Giants, or Red Sox. They labored for clubs called the Monarchs, Stars, Clowns, or Grays. Because of the unwritten and unfair code which segregated players, and leagues, into black and white, the players profiled in this book competed outside of organized baseball.

The term "Negro Leagues" refers to a loose group of all-black baseball squads established early in the twentieth century and which existed until the late 1950s. These clubs provided African-Americans an outlet and an opportunity to play and participate in "The National Pastime." The players endured long road trips in buses and automobiles, often playing in one town one day, and another town hundreds of miles away the next day. The Negro Leagues were essentially barnstorming clubs, that is, they were performers who played wherever they could find a paying audience Games, sometimes arranged on short notice to accomodate a local semi-pro team, sometimes took place on a country ballpark before a few hundred locals; but sometimes, as in the case of the All-Star Game, they could be played at major league stadiums rented for the occasion like Comiskey

Park in Chicago or Griffith Stadium in Washington, D.C., before crowds of fifty or sixty thousand fans.

Still, the world of the Negro Leaguer was a shadow world, pacing along just underneath and just behind the "legitimate" big leagues, which were all-white from 1898 until 1946. In an era before television, and before sports events were regularly broadcast even on radio, when baseball was *the* game, and almost any boy knew the rosters of such white clubs as the New York Yankees or the St. Louis Cardinals, the Negro Leaguer was a hero, or known at all, only to that part of the population that was black. Only black-owned newspapers such as the *Pittsburgh Courier*, the *Baltimore Afro-American*, and the *Chicago Defender* carried accounts of the games, and these were often in the form of summaries rather than box scores.

But the level of play was very high, and the greatest stars accumulated legends by word of mouth. Enough fans, including some white ones, had seen, and been mesmerized by, the exploits of players like Josh Gibson and Leroy "Satchel" Paige, that national magaines such as *Time*, or *The Sporting News*, would devote some space to them. And, slowly, some people began asking the question: why are not these great players given the universal acclaim and respect they deserve?

But, by and large, the greatness of Negro Leagues players existed in the memories of fans who had seen them in person, and especially in the memories of the players who played against them. Photographs are scant, films virtually nonexistent. The sports writer, the biographer, must take the word of the men who were there and saw what happened.

Fortunately, in 1947, baseball's color barrier came tumbling down, when the great Jackie Robinson (who had briefly played in the Negro Leagues) took the field for the Brooklyn Dodgers. Scores of black ballplayers eventually found their way to major league rosters.

Unfortunately, an entire nation soon forgot or ignored the heritage the Negro Leagues left behind. But, by the 1970s, and after many other struggles for equal rights had been won, the ripple of interest in black baseball grew into a gigantic wave. The Baseball Hall of Fame formed a special committee to study the Negro Leagues and recommend former players for enshirement. Their efforts were hampered because many records had been lost, and numerous players, witnesses to this or that feat of skill, had passed on. But, over the next decade, a consensus was reached, and some of the very greatest of the Negro League stars received long-overdue recognition.

Blackball Superstars spins the stories of a mere dozen Negro League heroes recognized in Cooperstown since 1971. Several other inductees are not included in the book, notably Martin Dihingo, a versatile star who played in the Negro Leagues but whose main career was spent in the baseball leagues of Mexico and Latin America; and Monte Irvin, a Negro Leagues veteran who played most of his career in the big leagues. The authors sincerely hope that more of these African-American stars will be inducted to the Hall of Fame in the future. More importantly, we want the lessons of faith and perseverance exhibited in these pages to inspire and uplift our readers.

A word should be said here about the futility of trying to compare stars from different eras who played in different leagues against different competition. It is tempting, for instance, to try to compare Josh Gibson, the great Negro League power hitter, with Babe Ruth, the Yankee slugger and home-run king, and to ask "Who was best?" Gibson was even called the "Black Babe Ruth" in his own day. Had he played in the major leagues, would Gibson have bested Ruth's long-standing record of 60 home runs in a season? Would he, indeed, have set home run records the current home run lifetime leader, Hank Aaron, could not have reached? We will never know. The only thing that can be fairly said is that both men were unequalled during the time they played, and against the best competition available to them. Ruth played in the major leagues; Gibson played in the Negro Leagues. Both are rightfully where they belong now, in the National Baseball Hall of Fame.

Ace Collins

John Hillman

BLACKBALL SUPERSTARS

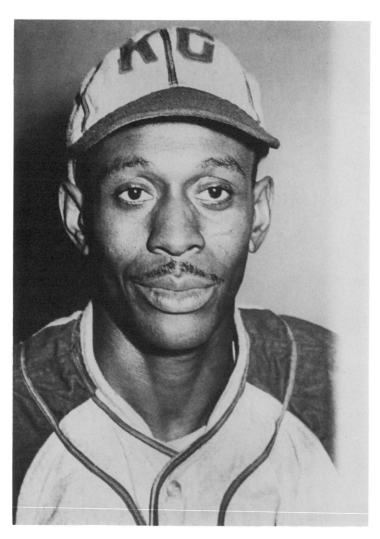

Leroy "Satchel" Paige

Leroy "Satchel" Paige

Don't look back. Something might be gaining on you—Satchel Paige's rule number six for staying young.

Leroy "Satchel" Paige and television would have paired perfectly. The slender, right-handed pitcher combined the power of Roger Clemens, the flash of Michael Jordan, the banter of Muhammad Ali, and the outrageousness of Dennis Rodman.

Paige threw hard and described his pitches with color and flair. Opposing batters and fans witnessed the "Midnight Creeper," the "Four-Day Rider," the "Two-Hump Blooper," the "Bat Dodger," the "Hesitation Pitch," and most often the "Be-Ball." Satchel called the "Be-Ball" his favorite because, "it goes where I want it to be."

In reality, his arsenal consisted almost entirely of fastballs. But in using this one pitch, the six-foot, three-inch hurler nipped and carved the strike zone with a surgeon's precision.

Hall of Fame first baseman Walter "Buck" Leonard best described Satch's pitching: "He threw fire. The ball would get up to the plate and rise just a little, just enough for you to miss it."

Even as a youngster in Mobile, Alabama, the future fireballer garnered center stage. As a seven-year-old, he rigged a pole with ropes to haul bags at the train station for pocket money. Another porter observed, "You look like a walking satchel tree." The nickname stuck. Leroy Paige died, and "Satchel" Paige was born.

His birth officially occurred on July 7, 1906. Satchel, the seventh of 11 children, grew up in a typical turn-of-the-century black household. He accepted ragged clothes, meager food, and sub-standard housing as facts rather than choices. But early on Paige discovered a talent to carry him away from a dead-end existence. The black boy could hurl rocks harder and faster than anyone in South Alabama.

Satchel first used his skill to kill chickens for supper. He advanced to slaying ducks on the fly. The king of the rock throwers eventually threw well-placed strikes against human competition.

Wilbur Hines, baseball coach at W. H. Council School, channeled Satchel's talent from the street to the mound. By age ten, Paige had established a reputation as a hard-throwing righthander. But Hines couldn't keep his young protege in line. The impetuous youth shoplifted some cheap rings at age twelve. The local truant officer administered swift justice and assigned Satchel to the Industrial School for Negro Children at Mount Meigs, near Montgomery.

Reform school turned into a blessing for the wayward boy. Paige received basic schooling, participated in choir and band, and played baseball. Coaches gave the gangly teenager valuable pitching tips.

Satchel returned to Mobile five years later and found little change there. Poverty lingered, and his family struggled to make ends meet. His mother implored the 17-year-old to seek steady employment.

Though he tried hard, the reform school graduate found no offers. Since his brother, Wilson, played for the semi-pro Mobile Tigers, Satchel earned a try-out with the team. Paige blew ten swinging strikes past the manager and signed for a bonus of one dollar.

For the next two years, Satchel pitched for pocket money in the Mobile semi-pro leagues. Legends grew up around him as the former troublemaker tallied victory after victory. Paige didn't win games in a plain vanilla fashion, but fashioned them with pizzazz. In one game, while seeking his 26th consecutive victory, Paige held a 1-0 lead with two out in the bottom of the ninth. Then three straight errors loaded the bases.

The crowd booed. Their razzing angered Satchel. To quiet their voices, the pitcher ordered his outfielders to sit on the grass behind the mound. The booing stopped, and soon the stadium buzzed with excitement. Paige fired the ball. Strike one! Strike two! Strike three! Satchel had won the game, and the crowd was now cheering.

Shortly after this incredible display of grace and skill, Satchel signed professionally with the Chattanooga Black Lookouts of the Negro Southern League. After chugging into Chattanooga, Paige moved up to the Birmingham Black Barons, the Nashville Elite Giants, and finally the Cleveland Cubs of the Negro National League.

During the 1931 campaign, owner Gus Greenlee enticed the fastball artist to jump to his newly formed club, the Pittsburgh Crawfords. Greenlee, who operated a popular nightspot called the Crawford Grill, had already assembled the best black baseball talent in the country. Paige joined an ensemble that included future Hall of Famers Oscar

Charleston, "Judy" Johnson, Josh Gibson, and James "Cool Papa" Bell.

But Satchel didn't confine his talents solely to the Crawfords. Every winter Paige traveled south of the border into Mexico to pitch in the winter leagues. And in the early spring, the righthander and a cast of Negro Leaguers toured the South and West of the United States. Often the Satchel Paige All-Stars engaged major league barnstorming teams. Praises for Satchel's fastball abounded from famous white players such as Hack Wilson, Jimmy Foxx, Rogers Hornsby, and pitcher Dizzy Dean.

Dean wrote in a Chicago newspaper, "I know who's the best pitcher I've ever seen, and it's old Satchel Paige. He sure is a pistol. It's too bad those colored boys don't play in the big leagues because they sure got some great ball players. Anyway, that skinny old Satchel Paige with those long arms is my idea of the pitcher with the greatest stuff I ever saw."

With his untiring work ethic, Paige always earned more money than any of his black contemporaries, sometimes incurring their jealousy as well as their admiration. But his flamboyant, money-spending lifestyle and marriage to Janet Howard led to a salary dispute with Greenlee.

When the Crawford owner refused to raise his

pay, the slender ace accepted an offer from Bismarck, North Dakota car dealer Neil Churchill to pitch for his white semi-pro team. There, Satchel won a staggering 134 of 150 games against differing levels of competition. Paige's prairie club captured the first National Baseball Congress tournament in Wichita, Kansas. Their star pitcher struck out 60 batters in four games and walked away with the Most Valuable Player award.

In the spring of 1937, Dominican Republic president Rafael Trujillo offered Paige and seven other Crawfords $30,000 to play for his Cuidad Trujillo team. The Dominicans already had a great baseball tradition, and were some of the game's most emotional fans That year, the championship game against Estrellas de Oriente resembled a Hollywood movie scene. Barefooted but heavily armed soldiers surrounded the diamond in support of the dictator's team. Paige's manager told him to win the game, or else face a revolution, and perhaps execution. But Trujillo's frightened hired players were able to win 6-5, and Satchel bade farewell forever to the island nation.

Still angry over Satchel's earlier abandonment, Gus Greenlee sold his contract to Effa Manley's Newark Eagles. But Paige, always independent and perhaps petulant that Mrs. Manley had spurned his romantic advances, never reported to Newark, and traveled south to play again in the Mexican League.

Satchel was overworked in Mexico, and developed a sore arm. Needing the money, he continued to pitch through his pain. The aching grew worse until the rubber-armed pitcher could no longer throw.

Doctors predicted Paige would never hurl a baseball again. But J. L. Wilkinson, owner of the Kansas City Monarchs, took a chance. He acquired the rights to the wounded righthander and assigned him to the alternate traveling squad. Wilkinson believed Paige would draw crowds even if his performance had suffered.

Satchel slowly worked his injured limb into shape. The pain disappeared, and the fastball reappeared. The old Paige had been reborn.

The Monarchs and the revived righthander formed a successful partnership unparalleled in the Negro Leagues. For almost a decade, Satchel pitched the Kansas City club to championship after championship.

In 1942, the Monarchs faced Satch's former team, the Pittsburgh Crawfords, in the Negro League World Series. During a crucial game, Kansas City led in the top of the seventh when Pittsburgh's Jerry Benjamin belted a triple. Paige called his first baseman John "Buck" O'Neil over for a conference.

"You know what I'm fixing to do?" the showboating pitcher confessed. "I'm going to put Vic Harris on base. Then I'm going to put Howard Easterling on base. And then I'm going to pitch to Josh Gibson."

The shocked O'Neil returned to his position, shaking his head. Eight straight balls later, Satchel faced Gibson, a legendary slugger called the "Babe Ruth of the Negro Leagues."

The king of the hill eyed Gibson warily and stepped off the mound. He motioned for a bicarbonate of soda to settle his stomach (a piece of showmanship that nevertheless helped Paige, as his stomach was his weakest part). Paige downed the drink and let out a loud belch. The crowd howled with glee.

Satch toed the rubber and fired his "be-ball." Gibson never took the bat off his shoulder.

"Okay, Josh," the hurler taunted. "Now I'm going to throw you another fastball, just about the same place. But it's going to be a little harder than the last one."

Paige threw the "midnight creeper" with wild abandon. The umpire bellowed, "Strike two!"

"Josh," Satch shouted. "I'm going to smoke your

yolk. Here comes my 'four-day rider'."

Boom! The ball thundered into the catcher's mitt for strike three. Gibson, perhaps psychologically beaten by Paige's bravado, had not swung at a single pitch.

In the off-season, the master of control continued to hire out for exhibitions whenever possible. Paige pitched on virtually every baseball diamond from Canada to South America. Handbills advertised, "Satchel Paige, the World's Greatest Pitcher — Guaranteed to Strike Out the First Nine Men!" The righthander seldom failed to come close to his promise.

With Jackie Robinson breaking the major leaue color barrier in 1947, other talented blacks were certain to follow into the major leagues. Some thought Satchel would be a natural for the big leagues, but at age 42, it was unsure if the old master could win in the majors.

In 1948, Cleveland Indian owner Bill Veeck needed pitching help for the tight pennant race with the Boston Red Sox and New York Yankees. His friend, Abe Saperstein, owner of basketball's Harlem Globetrotters, recommended Satchel. In a secret tryout, the aging hurler threw 60 pitches. Fifty-six found the strike zone, and Veeck was impressed enough to offer a contract. Though baseball's Bible, *The Sporting News*, dismissed the signing as a publicity stunt, Paige quickly proved them wrong.

On July 9th, Indians field manager Lou Boudreau summoned Paige from the bullpen to relieve Bob Lemon. Satchel slowly ambled to the mound. His performance didn't set the world on fire, but he hurled two shutout innings and allowed only two hits. It was only after this initial outing that the pressure of being the major leagues' first black pitcher subsided. Still, it took almost a month for the Indians to bring him to center stage.

The former Negro League ace appeared eight times in relief, then finally drew a start. On August 2nd, Satchel made baseball history; seventy-two thousand Cleveland supporters packed Municipal Stadium and witnessed the event. Paige struggled, but the powerful Indian bats forged a 5-3 lead. Ed Klieman relieved in the eighth and nailed down Satchel's victory. One of baseball's best pitchers had finally won a major league game.

Boudreau used his 42-year-old hurler wisely for the pennant stretch run. Paige started six crucial games and relieved in a dozen more. Paige's six wins, including two shutouts, helped propel the Indians into their first World Series in 28 years.

Satchel returned to the majors for a season in 1949, but his pitching was only mediocre. The departure of Bill Veeck left the hurler homeless in 1950. He returned to the world of barnstorming with its long car trips, small town crowds, and marathon appearances. As the ageless black pitcher showcased his arm across America, the New York Giants and Boston Braves made overtures about his returning to organized baseball. But Satchel turned them down

In mid-July 1951, Veeck purchased the hapless, last place St. Louis Browns. Eight days later, the 45-year-old hurler reunited with the eccentric showman.

As the Browns were perennial American League cellar dwellers, Veeck and Paige combined for more laughs than victories. The maverick owner used every promotion imaginable, including a dwarf as a pinch-hitter, to attract fans. He even installed a rocking chair in the bullpen for the ageless Satchel to await his summons to the mound.

But after two and a half years even the wildest promotion no longer worked. Lagging attendance ended the Veeck regime in St. Louis. A Maryland investor group bought the Browns, relocated the team to Baltimore, and renamed the club the Orioles.

Paige faced unemployment once more. He toured for one season with Abe Saperstein and another with the Monarchs. But it seemed time to hang up the cleats forever. But Satchel could hardly imagine a life without baseball.

Again, the wild and crazy Bill Veeck rode to the rescue. As the new vice-president of the International League's Miami Marlins, he signed the former Indian and Brown. At the age of a half-century, Paige finished the 1956 season as the league's top pitcher.

With Veeck's departure the following year, relations between the Marlins and the ageless wonder grew cool. After an acting fling in *The Wonderful Country* with Robert Mitchum and Julie London, Paige returned to his tried and true calling, touring with his all-star baseball team. Although the pickings were slim, Midwest fans turned out in strong numbers to see the legendary control artist one more time.

In the 1960s, Paige appeared less and less. Many had forgotten him altogether. One major league owner still recalled the old man's drawing power. Publicity hungry Charlie Finley signed the forever-young pitcher for a one-game contract in late September 1965.

Satchel started for the last-place Kansas City

Athletics against the Boston Red Sox. As old as he was, the 2,000-game winner could still strut his stuff. He threw three shutout innings, allowing future Hall of Famer Carl Yastrzemski the only hit.

On July 5, 1982, Kansas City dedicated a $250,000 facility called the Satchel Paige Memorial Stadium. "Nobody on earth could feel as I do now," the Negro League veteran remarked. Emphysema killed him three days later at age 75.

Satchel Paige brought the Negro Leagues from the darkness into the light. More than any other players, he and Josh Gibson were known by black and white fans alike to be more than worthy of playing in the major leagues. Their talent, notoriety and fan appeal could not forever be denied.

The National Baseball Hall of Fame and Museum inducted Leroy "Satchel" Paige on August 9, 1971, along with Chick Haley, Harry Hooper, Rube Marquard, Dave Bancroft, Jake Beckley, and Joe Kelley. The special committee on Negro League baseball selected the legendary righthander as the first honoree.

Paige received thunderous applause when he took the podium. The pitcher's opening statement brought howls of laughter from the crowd.

"Since I've been here I've heard myself called some very nice names," Satchel said. "And I can remember when some of the men in there called me some ba-a-a-d names, when I used to pitch against them."

Paige turned serious and sentimental as he concluded his remarks. "I am the proudest man on earth today, and my wife and sister and sister-in-law and son all feel the same. It's a wonderful day and one who appreciates it is Leroy "Satchel" Paige."

Joshua "Josh" Gibson

Joshua "Josh" Gibson

If Josh Gibson had been in the big leagues in his time, Babe Ruth and Hank Aaron would still be chasing him for the home run record.—Hall of Fame third baseman William "Judy" Johnson

Josh Gibson, the man who would become black baseball's most feared power hitter, was born on December 21, 1911 near the small hamlet of Buena Vista in southwest Georgia. It was a poor, rural place with litle opportunity. In 1923, his father Mark left to find work in the coal and iron industry in Pittsbirgh, Pennsylvania. Three years later, he was able to bring his family north to join him.

As a boy, Gibson watched his father return from the Carnegie-Illinois steel mill. Each day, the man slowly labored homeward from the hot, hard, tedious, backbreaking work that sapped his strength.

Despite the hardships, Josh knew Pittsburgh's North Side bettered their previous life. Before migrating to the Steel City, their small family plot of Georgia clay provided an existence and nothing more. In later years, the Hall of Famer would proclaim, "The greatest gift Dad gave me was to get me out of the South."

In the North's Promised Land, Gibson received a modest education. He dropped out of Allegheny Pre-Vocational School after completing the ninth grade. The youth apprenticed at theWestinghouse Air Brake Company, but his true devotion focused on sports, not work. Eventually, the teenager left Westinghouse to work and play ball for the Gimbel Brothers Department Store. He was a standout for the company's black team, the Gimbel Brothers A.C.

Harold Tinker, centerfielder for the semi-pro Pittsburgh Crawford Colored Giants, noticed Gibson's powerful swing and sturdy catcher's build. He convinced the young man to join Pittsburgh..

"He became a tremendous success," Tinker recalled. "He hit balls out on Bedford Avenue. He was actually the most tremendous hitter I've ever come across in baseball — I'm barring none."

Within a year and a half, Gibson was catching for the top black baseball club in the City of the Three Rivers, the Homestead Grays. A contest between the Kansas City Monarchs and the Grays played on July 25, 1930, was to show a spotlight on Josh that began a 17-year partnership between the player and Pittsburgh's black professional baseball.

The Monarchs' new portable lighting system allowed Forbes Field to host the first night game in the stadium's history. The erratic illumination created problems for the hometown team, but provided Gibson with the opportunity of a lifetime.

Homestead manager William "Judy" Johnson remembered the incident.

Joe Williams was pitching that night, and we didn't know anything about lights. We'd never played under them before, and we couldn't use the regular catcher's signals, because if he put his glove down you couldn't see it. So we used the glove straight up for a fastball and the glove down — that was supposed to be the curve. Some way Joe Williams and the catcher Buck Ewing got crossed up. The catcher was expecting the curve, and Joe threw the fast and caught him right there, and split the finger. Well, my other catcher was Vic Harris, and he was playing the outfield and couldn't catch. So Josh was sitting in the grandstand, and I asked the Grays' owner, Cum Posey, to get him to finish the game.

Posey approached the youth. He asked simply, "Josh, can you fill in behind the plate tonight?" The teenager fumbled for words and finally stammered, "Yeah, oh yeah!"

Posey motioned toward the clubhouse and told the equipment manager to outfit his new catcher. In a flash, the 19-year-old shed his clothes and donned a shirt with GRAYS emblazoned across the front.

The six-foot, one-inch, teenager caught the entire game without error. His performance and presence impressed Posey, and the owner offered Gibson a permanent position.

Although the young backstop possessed great potential, his receiving skills needed considerable improvement. He honed his glove work by catching batting practice before each game. Teammate Jimmie Crutchfield described the future Hall of Famer's defensive abilities:

"I can remember when he couldn't catch this building if you threw it at him. He was only behind the plate because of his hitting. And I watched him develop into a very good defensive catcher. He was never given enough credit for his ability as a catcher. They couldn't deny that he was a great hitter, but they could deny that he was a great catcher. But I know!"

The gentle giant could hit. Although newspapers called Gibson "the Black Babe Ruth," the only similarity existed in their quantity of home runs.

Ruth hit from the left side, and the Yankee outfielder swung from his heels and uppercut the ball. His homers tantalized fans with their slow arcing rise and fall. Gibson batted right and resembled a Jimmie Foxx, a Henry Aaron, a Willie Mays, or a Juan Gonzalez at the plate with his short, sweet, powerful punch. The Grays' catcher hit screaming line drives. Spectators gasped as the ball rocketed off the bat.

But, even as the slugging catcher sparkled on the field, his personal life was ripping him apart. Josh had married Helen Mason, his 17-year-old sweetheart, but the teenage bride died in August 1930, tragically succumbing to complications from childbirth. Josh never recovered from his wife's death, becoming increasingly moody and solitary. Helen left her young husband with a set of fraternal twins, Josh, Jr. and Helen.

With no means of providing his family a livelihood except playing baseball, Gibson left his children with Helen's family. It was only when the twins grew older that the Negro League star devoted greater energy to their upbringing.

Josh, Jr. did later benefit from his father's exalted status. From age eight, he served as the Grays' batboy. During summer vacations, the youngster accompanied the team on road trips throughout Pennsylvania, West Virginia, Ohio, and New York.

Despite his time at the ballpark, Gibson's son felt distant from his father. He recalls, "My father was never home much because in those days, after the Negro Leagues finished playing ball in the United States, many of the players went to the Latin countries and played winter ball. It seemed I really got to know my father in the last year of his life. He didn't go away that winter; he was home all the time."

In his first full year with the Grays, Gibson clouted 75 home runs. Many came against semi-pro competition, but legends spread quickly about the soft-spoken catcher whose bat resounded like thunder.

Josh's reputation caught the ear of Gus Greenlee, owner of the well-known night club, the Crawford Grill. In 1932, Greenlee put together the best black team money could buy, the Crawfords. He brought established stars such as Satchel Paige and James "Cool Papa" Bell to Pittsburgh. Then he lured hometown heroes Oscar Charleston, Judy Johnson, and Gibson away from the Grays.

For five years, Pittsburgh's black population watched the nation's top baseball team. While they came to watch the team, it was Josh who often left the fans amazed. Gibson not only homered with regularity, his clouts defied imagination.

Although some baseball historians dispute the story, Jack Marshall, Chicago American Giant infielder, claims the power hitter blasted the only fair ball ever hit out of Yankee Stadium. "Josh hit the ball over that triple deck next to the bullpen in left field. Over and out! I will never forget that day," recalled Marshall.

In 1937, Greenlee suddenly lost interest in baseball as a business. With little warning, the Crawfords disbanded and Gibson returned to his original team, the Homestead Grays. Josh did delay his reunion by several months, traveling to the Dominican Republic to play along with Satchel Paige and other Negro Leaguers.

Led by their strong-armed catcher, the Grays dominated the Negro National League and the barnstorming circuit in the late 1930s. With a supporting cast of Buck Leonard, Sam Bankhead, and Vic Harris, the Homestead club remained on top even when Josh defected to the Mexican League in 1940.

It took two years for owner Posey and the wayward catcher to settle their contractual differences, and by 1942, Josh's talent was in decline. The once-solid teenager had ballooned to 230 pounds. Hours of constant crouching as a catcher had worn out the cartilage in his knees. Like his white alter ego Ruth, Josh was known to be a heavy drinker. He began to have violent headaches, which often limited his effectiveness, and served as a warning of dark days to come.

But the slugger was indeed ill. On New Year's Day 1943, Gibson blacked out and lapsed into a coma. Doctors diagnosed the cause as a brain tumor, but the black home run king refused surgery. Remarkably, he continued to play ball.

Josh's only concession to his physical problems was to curtail his catching. But reduced playing time couldn't halt the growth that ravaged his body.

On January 20, 1947, Gibson informed his mother he felt ill. As his family gathered around his bedside, the "Black Babe Ruth" suffered a stroke, and later died quietly in his sleep.

Like many, Gibson's chance for glory and fame in the big leagues never came. Josh died four months before Jackie Robinson would shatter baseball's color line.

On several occasions, the home run hitting catcher had stood at opportunity's door. But the lords of baseball refused to crack it open. Sports historians can only speculate how well Gibson might have fared in the major leagues.

The Pittsburgh Pirates and Washington Senators knew Josh well. Their owners often watched the black bomber hammer mammoth shots into the cavernous reaches of Forbes Field and Griffith Stadium. Second division clubs with distant left field fences would have improved instantly with Gibson's power. Yet, they refused to break an unwritten rule: "No blacks need apply."

Fortunately, wiser men finally destroyed the barrier. But Josh Gibson never lived to witness the walls come tumbling down.

The National Baseball Hall of Fame and Museum inducted Josh Gibson posthumously on August 7, 1972. His class included Yogi Berra, Lefty Gomez, Sandy Koufax, Early Wynn, and fellow Negro Leaguer, Buck Leonard. Ross Youngs and Will

Harridge were also posthumous inductees.

Gibson's son, Josh Jr., who played briefly in the Negro Leagues, gave the acceptance speech on behalf of his father. His brief remarks summed up a lifetime of frustration.

"I want to say a personal word to my father," the younger Gibson said. "Wake up, Dad, you just made it in."

From the Collection
of the National
Baseball Hall of Fame
Library and Archive

Walter "Buck" Leonard

Walter "Buck" Leonard

Buck Leonard could play baseball. He batted better than Lou Gehrig and fielded as smoothly as George Sisler or Hal Chase.— Author Brent Kelley

Life began for Buck Leonard on September 8, 1907, near the small North Carolina town of Rocky Mount. His father died when he was only 11 years old, and as the eldest of six children, he assumed the responsibility of providing for the family.

Leonard discovered baseball in 1921 when the city moved Municipal Stadium near his home. "I started looking through the fence to see the fellows play," Buck remembered. "We looked through the cracks until the police stopped us, and then we stood on boxes. The police told us that was illegal, too, but I really got hooked."

The orphaned boy dropped out of school at age 14 to work in a stocking mill. Shortly afterward, Leonard switched to shining shoes at the railway station.

In 1922, he joined the Atlantic Coast Line railroad as a shop employee. Buck filled his nights and weekends playing semi-pro baseball with various teams throughout North Carolina and Virginia.

The vagabond life continued for over a decade. He sharpened his hitting and fielding skills, waiting patiently for opportunity to knock.

Fate forced Leonard's hand in 1933. The railroad laid off the long-time employee along with dozens of others. The Great Depression held everyone tightly in its grasp. At age 26, Buck felt he should have known better than to try playing baseball professionally. But, he had no other way to earn even a few dollars

A scout named Ramirez contacted Leonard and asked the out-of-work first baseman about playing winter baseball in Puerto Rico. An all-star team of barnstormers would depart New York on November 15th. Since he had not worked for months, Buck immediately answered yes.

The day arrived, and the North Carolina native reported. Filled with dreams of tropical baseball, the young ballplayer learned painful news. The Puerto Rican roster had been reduced from 15 to 12, leaving no place for him. Leonard had no job, no prospects, and no place to turn. The rejected ballplayer returned to Rocky Mount uncertain what the future would hold, and again played for local semi-pro squads.

The next Spring, Ben Taylor, brother of Indianapolis ABC's manager C. I.Taylor, brought his Baltimore Stars to Portsmouth, Virginia. After engaging Leonard's semi-pro team, Taylor asked the journeyman ballplayer to join him.

The aging player-manager taught Buck the finer points of playing first base. Although he received valuable instruction, the traveling team experienced meager paydays. For weekday games, the team of Stars might net $20. Weekend contests produced slightly more, perhaps $50 or $75. After deducting food and lodging, individual players received only about $5 per week.

Fighting for his financial life, Taylor decided to take his team to New York, but bookings with other black teams never materialized. The Dumas Hotel sold their two cars to pay the rent. Finally giving up, the manager suggested his players return home as best they could.

Luckily, Buck earned a position with the Brooklyn Royal Giants and played the remainder of 1933 in New York.

The five-foot, 10-inch first baseman reported to the Royal Giants again in early April 1934. One night he visited a nightspot and met "Smoky" Joe Williams, pitcher for Pittsburgh's Homestead Grays.

Williams quizzed the ballplayer. "Look, Buck," the pitcher asked, "don't you want to get with a good team?"

"Sure," Leonard responded. "What are you talking about?"

"The Homestead Grays," Smoky answered back. "I'm going to call Cum Posey, the owner, tonight and see what he says. I've seen you play two or three times, and I think you can make the team."

Posey agreed and wired Leonard traveling money. The former Royal Giant left New York and headed for Wheeling, West Virginia. After a week of practice, Buck made the team. The relationship was to endure for 17 seasons.

The seasons stretched endlessly. "We'd play 200 to 210 games a year," the veteran admitted. "Then we'd go to Cuba or Puerto Rica and play winter ball."

Game days passed with scarcely a break. "We'd play a semi-pro team in Maryland in the afternoon and a league game in Griffith Stadium that night," Buck recalled.

Discrimination forced black teams to endure terrible conditions. "Sometimes we'd stay in hotels that had so many bedbugs you had to put a newspaper down between the mattress and the sheets," Leonard remarked. "Other times we'd rent rooms in a YMCA, or we'd go to a hotel and rent three rooms. That way you got the use of the bath."

When the Pittsburgh Crawfords disbanded in 1937, catcher Josh Gibson rejoined the Grays. The reacquisition helped propel the Homestead club to nine straight Negro National League championships. Sportswriters billed Gibson and Leonard as, "The Thunder Twins." Others referred to the duo as the "Black Babe Ruth" and the "Black Lou Gehrig."

With the catcher batting third and the first baseman hitting cleanup, the Grays boasted a powerful lineup. Gibson blasted home runs in record numbers, and Leonard punched line drives to all fields. Sketchy Negro League records list the North Carolina native's lifetime batting average as somewhere between .324 and .340. His season marks included .383 in 1940, .375 in 1945, .410 in 1947, and .395 in 1948.

Arguably the finest squad ever assembled might have been the 1948 Grays. Gibson had died the previous year, but Luke Easter, Sam Bankhead, Luis Marquez, Wilmer Fields, and Leonard provided powerful hitting and clutch pitching. That year, the Grays defeated the Birmingham Black Barons, led by a 15-year-old centerfielder named Willie Mays, for their third Negro World Series championship.

Still, the '48 title marked the end of an era. As the major leagues signed black players in greater and greater numbers, black fans shifted their allegiance, and the Negro Leagues faded into oblivion.

With the demise of black baseball in 1950, the veteran Leonard journeyed south to the Mexican League. He spent three years with Torreon and two in Durango. Bill Veeck, owner of the St. Louis Browns, offered Leonard a shot at the major leagues in 1952, but Buck refused, stating that at age 45 he was simply too old.

The Pittsburgh stalwart never expressed bitterness about missed opportunities. He accepted exclusion as a product of the times. "[Washington Senators owner] Clark Griffith said our league wasn't organized," Leonard commented. "We were organized, but we weren't recognized. There was a lot of racism. Sometimes it was frustrating, but I think it made us play better. We couldn't play with whites back then. So we just went out and played ball and tried to show everyone that we were just as good."

When the long-time Pittsburgh standout retired from baseball in 1955, he returned to Rocky Mount and worked as a truant officer. He couldn't put baseball completely in the past, however. In 1962, Buck helped organized the Carolina League Rocky Mount Leafs.

Leonard suffered a stroke in 1984. Showing his grit and determination, he learned to write with his left hand in order to honor the countless autograph requests that came his way.

In 1994, the National League and the city of Pittsburgh recognized Buck's lifelong contribution to baseball. He served as the National League's honorary captain at the annual All-Star game held at Three Rivers Stadium.

The 12-time Negro League all-star died November 27, 1997, at age 90.

Walter "Buck" Leonard and Josh Gibson entered the National Baseball Hall of Fame and Museum as the second and third members chosen by the Negro League Committee. The ceremonies took place on August 7, 1972. Other inductees that year included Yogi Berra, Lefty Gomez, Sandy Koufax, Early Wynn, Ross Youngs, and Will Harridge.

Leonard expressed wonder at his selection for

Cooperstown, when at one time he couldn't even take the field alongside his white contemporaries. "But we felt we were contributing something to baseball, too," he said. "We played with a round ball and round bats, and we loved it and liked to play — because there wasn't much money in it. My getting in is something I never thought would happen."

From the Col...
of the National
Baseball Hall of Fame
Library and Archive

James "Cool Papa" Bell

James "Cool Papa" Bell

If Cool Papa had known about colleges, or if colleges had known about Cool Papa, Jesse Owens would have looked like he was walking.— Leroy "Satchel" Paige

Born May 17, 1903, James "Cool Papa" Bell grew up on a small corn and cotton farm near Starkville, Mississippi, about 75 miles from Tupelo, later the birthplace of Elvis Presley, "The King of Rock and Roll."

In 1920, the country boy joined his four brothers in St. Louis and played for the amateur Compton Hill Cubs. Two years later, tired of inconsistent paydays, Bell considered quitting baseball, but a timely opportunity knocked. The East St. Louis Cubs needed a pitcher to face the St. Louis Stars in an exhibition contest and requested the youngster's services. The lefthanded knuckleballer lost the game, 8-1, but struck out eight batters. The Stars thought he was a good prospect and offered him a contract for $90 a month. Bell turned professional.

Manager Bill Gatewood used his new acquisition sparingly. He told the 19-year-old to study the competition and learn their pitching techniques. That was good advice, for trickery abounded in the Negro Leagues. Batters faced a variety of unusual and sometimes "doctored" pitches: the spitball, the screwball, the emery ball, the shine ball, the mud ball, and the knuckle ball. Hurlers broke their pitches inside, outside, up, down, and all around.

Contrary to popular belief, Elvis Presley, James Dean, or Arthur Fonzarelli didn't invent "cool." Nor did Chuck Berry, Little Richard, James Brown, Ella Fitzgerald, or Lena Horne. The man who invented "cool" discovered the trait through a combination of luck and talent. In a moment that thousands would never forget, "cool" made its way into the game played on hot summer days.

St. Louis manager Gatewood decided the time had arrived to test his rookie pitcher. The Indianapolis ABCs had already beaten the Stars twice in a series and led in game three by a wide margin. The power-packed lineup of Ben Taylor, Oscar Charleston, Biz Mackey, and Crush Holloway had battered the St. Louis pitching staff without mercy. A new putcher was needed in relief.

The skipper asked new pitcher James Bell if he was nervous. The 19-year-old youngster replied, "Don't worry about me. I've pitched before big crowds in the sandlots."

His teammates marveled. "That boy sure is a cool one," they gasped. But the southpaw calmly strolled to the mound and struck out the stars Taylor and Charleston. Gatewood responded, "Yes sir, he's one cool papa." In an instant, the teenager had earned his lifelong nickname, "Cool Papa."

Through observation and practice, the slender lefthander quickly learned an assortment of curve balls, knuckle balls, and screwballs to keep the opposition hitters off-balance. His timely hitting positioned him in centerfield on the days he didn't pitch. Bell's blazing footspeed and consistent hitting finally convinced Gatewood to move the junkball pitcher to the outfield permanently in 1924.

Although the Mississippi native lacked home run power, his fleet feet turned singles into doubles and doubles into inside-the-park home runs. A walk to Bell resulted in a pair of stolen bases. A ball bounced to an infielder created more action than a troupe of acrobats. His teammates were heard to say, "he was so quiet, he was sudden."

Legends of Bell's daring on the basepaths grew

each year. Cool Papa frequently scored from first on a base hit to the outfield. It was claimed that a ball punched up the middle did not reach the outfielder until Bell slid into second base. Others recounted how baseball's fastest player stole two bases on one pitch. In an exhibition game against Bob Lemon's all-stars, the King of Thieves motored home from first base on a bunt.

Shortstop Bill Yancey saw Bell in his prime. He recalled:

I haven't seen anybody yet who could run with Cool. When I was on the Lincoln Giants, we played in a little park in New York called the Catholic Protectory up in the Bronx. That was our regular home field. Judy Johnson had been telling me about his guy that came to Cuba every winter, and Judy told me, if this guy hits the ball on two hops on the ground, you won't be able to throw him out from shortstop. Now I could throw, and I said nobody can outrun a baseball.

So the first time Cool Papa came to New York with the St. Louis Stars, he hit a ball into right field. Chino Smith was out there, and he could field a ball, and if you made a wide turn at first base he could throw you out trying to hustle back. I went out to get the throw, and when I looked up Cool Papa was slowing up going into third. And I said to myself, that sonofagun didn't touch second. Next time up he hit another one about the same place. Now, nobody got a three-base hit in that little park, I don't care where they hit the ball. And I watched this guy run. Well, he came across second base and it looked like his feet weren't touching the ground!

And he never argued, never said anything. That was why they called him Cool Papa; he was a real gentleman."

The speedy outfielder stayed with the Stars through 1931. Then when the Great Depression forced the St. Louis club and the entire Negro National League into bankruptcy, Bell joined the Detroit Senators. When the Motor City club also collapsed in mid-season, Cool Papa headed south and hooked up with the Kansas City Monarchs.

In 1933, Gus Greenlee's hefty bankroll lured Bell to the Pittsburgh Crawfords. Joined by Satchel Paige, Josh Gibson, Judy Johnson, and Oscar Charleston, the speed demon stayed in Steeltown until 1938. During the 1937 campaign, he detoured to the Dominican Republic with Paige and seven other Crawfords to play for President Rafael Trujillo. Bell enjoyed south-of-the-border baseball so much he returned the next year. From 1938 to 1941, he remained in the Mexican League, playing with Tampico, Torreon, Veracruz, and Monterrey.

Mr. Cool came home to the United States in 1942, and signed with the Chicago American Giants. But Cum Posey, owner of the Homestead Grays, convinced Bell to head back to Pittsburgh the following year. Teaming with Josh Gibson, Buck Leonard, Sam Bankhead, and Vic Harris, the speedy centerfielder led the Grays to back-to-back Negro World Series championships in 1943 and 1944.

Creeping arthritis slowed Cool Papa down in the post-war era. His bat still banged out hit after hit, but his legs lacked their former racehorse speed. He retired as an active player after the 1946 campaign.

In 1948, Satchel Paige offered his former teammate the helm of the Kansas City Monarchs "B" team. Paige supposedly told Bell he would receive a finder's fee for any major league prospects he signed. But, though "Cool Papa" discovered Elston Howard, Ernie Banks, and over a dozen other quality players, no money ever changed hands.

Bell's disappointment with the Monarchs job disillusioned him with baseball. Even when the St. Louis Browns offered the ex-Negro Leaguer a contract in 1951, he refused to sign, stating he could no longer perform up to standards.

Even though he declined the Browns offer, the ex-star setled in St. Louis and joined the municipal workforce. He retired after 21 years service as a custodian and night watchman.

In the 1970s, St. Louis recognized their adopted son for his lifetime of Negro League achievement. The city fathers renamed Dickson Street, Bell's address for 35 years, as James "Cool Papa" Bell Avenue.

Cool Papa harbored no ill will toward organized baseball for shunning Negro Leaguers. He explained, "I've got no kicks, no regrets. Of course it would have been nice to play in the majors, but I have my memories. I'm not the guy who wants to be praised too much. I never wanted to be a big shot. I don't have enough money to go around to those places where an outstanding guy should go. I know what I did, and I'm satisfied."

The star of a bygone era suffered a heart attack on February 27, 1991. He died a week later at the age of 87.

James "Cool Papa" Bell received induction to the National Baseball Hall of Fame and Museum on August 12, 1974. The honored ex-players included Bell, Mickey Mantle, Whitey Ford, Jocko Conlan, Sam Thompson, and Jim Bottomley. Satchel Paige, Roy Campanella, Buck Leonard, and Monte Irvin journeyed to Cooperstown to attend the ceremony.

Baseball commissioner Bowie Kuhn introduced the Negro League standout and apologized for his exclusion from organized baseball. "Through no fault of his own, he never played in the big leagues," Kuhn stated.

Bell expressed gratitude and appreciation for his enshrinement. "There were a lot of great ones in the Negro Leagues," he said. "We — Satchel, Irvin, Campy, Leonard, and myself — were the lucky ones. I'm thanking God for letting me smell the roses while I'm still living."

William Julius "Judy" Johnson

William Julius "Judy" Johnson

Judy, it's a darn shame you weren't a white boy because you could sign your own contract. —Philadelphia Athletics owner and manager Connie Mack

William Julius Johnson was born in Snow Hill, Maryland, on October 26, 1899. At age six, the Johnson family moved to Wilmington, Delaware, where Judy made his llfelong home. The young black boy inherited a strong sports tradition from his father; the head of the Johnson clan worked on the docks by day and served part-time as the athletic director for the Negro Settlement Home. He encouraged his son to box, but the future Hall of Famer preferred the baseball diamond to the boxing ring.

From the time the youngster could throw a ball or swing a bat, he hung out on the sandlots. Around the age of 14, Johnson joined the Rosedales, an organized team who played on Saturdays. No one received pay, but fans pitched in pocket change to buy new baseballs.

By 1918, the World War I military draft had claimed some of black baseball's top professionals. The 18-year-old Johnson, not drafted, was ready to step up to take their place.

The Hilldale club, based in Darby, a Philadelphia suburb, signed the Wilmington native for five dollars a game. On Thursdays and Saturdays, the Hilldales played in Darby. On Sundays, the team traveled to Atlantic City, switched uniforms, and billed themselves as the Bacharach Giants. This was a standard practice for black teams at the time.

After the war, when the top players returned from service, Johnson gained experience with the Madison Stars, a team with close ties to Hilldale. A year later, his skills finely tuned, owner Ed Boulden brought the third baseman to Darby permanently.

Boulden fostered stability for the Hilldales, something unknown to most Negro League teams. The well-kept ballpark seated 5,000 and drew black and white fans alike. Johnson recalled, "Our crowds got so big we had to enlarge the park—not just for Negroes, for white fans too. The A's and Phillies (Philadelphia's white pro teams) weren't doing very well then, and people were getting season tickets to see us. You couldn't buy a box seat."

Because the club had achieved financial security, Boulden paid his players a regular salary rather than a percentage of the gate, the norm at the time. Johnson started at $115 per month, but by 1929 was earning an almost unimaginable $250 salary.

Philadelphia's central location reduced travel times and distances for Hilldale. Competition from semi-pro teams both black and white abounded in the area. Baltimore and New York sites could be reached in an hour's drive. On rare occasions, the Hilldales looped from Pittsburgh to Chicago, Detroit, St.Louis and back. But, the team concentrated most of their efforts in and around Philadelphia.

Judy married his long-time sweetheart, school-teacher Anita T. Irons, in 1923, and appreciated being able to stay close to home. Playing for the Hilldales meant Johnson spent many nights in his own house, while other Negro Leaguers endured long road trips and stays in fourth-rate hotels.

For Judy, a hiring of major significance to his career marked 1923. John Henry "Pop" Lloyd took over as manager for the Hilldales. The slick-fielding shortstop instructed Johnson on some of baseball's finer points of glovework. Judy remembers how the future Hall of Famer trained him: "Lloyd was a great teacher; he'd make you play your head off, and he was always full of encouragement."

During his days under Lloyd, teammates decided Johnson bore a strong resemblance to a veteran player named Robert "Judy" Gans. They began calling their young star, "Judy." Following the Negro League tradition, the novice third baseman adopted the unusual label and answered to it the rest of his life.

The Darby ballclub experienced great success during Johnson's early years, capturing the Eastern Colored League crown in 1923, 1924, and 1925.

In 1924, the Negro League team began a long tradition when they engaged the Kansas City Monarchs, champions of the Negro National League, in the Negro League World Series. The two clubs would meet again for the title in 1925.

With fan interest high in all points of the east and the midwest, the teams wisely chose playing sites for the Series in Philadelphia, Baltimore, Chicago, and Kansas City. The Monarchs captured the first inter-league matchup, but the Hilldales exacted revenge by winning the second a year later.

In 1924, the American League's Philadelphia

Athletics challenged the Darby club to a three game post-season exhibition series. When the Hilldales swept their white counterparts, baseball commissioner Kenesaw Mountain Landis forbade major league clubs from playing Negro League teams. Only traveling white all-star squads could face black teams and risk humiliation.

The A's series impacted Johnson for many years to come. Philadelphia owner and manager Cornelius McGillicuddy, better known as Connie Mack, befriended the black third baseman every time he got the chance.

Impressed by his talent, Mack issued the Negro League star a free pass to Shibe Park, allowing Judy to spend every off-day studying the play of Athletic third baseman Jimmie Dykes. The opportunity to observe major leaguers up close was a learning experience Judy took to heart. He not only added knowledge to his own game, he discovered firsthand his skills were equal to those in the "Bigs."

As the 1920s came to a close, John Drew acquired the Hilldales. Despite the new ownership and added capital, hard economic times at the start of the Great Depression forced the team into bankruptcy.

In 1930, Johnson relocated to Pittsburgh and

joined the Homestead Grays. Though only 29 years old, he assumed the manager's role in addition to playing third base. During his managerial tenure, the Grays signed young catcher Josh Gibson. Johnson spent hours tutoring the youngster, who would become a great star, in the art of catching. Judy recalled, "He used to catch batting practice for me and then catch the game. He really wanted to learn. He was the biggest kid you ever saw in your life. Oh, he was jolly all the time and very sensitive."

Gus Greenlee lured the all-star third baseman from the Grays to his newly formed Pittsburgh Crawfords in 1932. Other stars followed. The Crawfords were to rule the Negro Leagues in the 1930s with their Hall of Fame lineup. At one time, Greenlee's club fielded five of Coopertown's elite: Satchel Paige, Josh Gibson, Oscar Charleston, James "Cool Papa" Bell, and Johnson.

The Crawfords paid top wages, but the players earned every penny. The 1932 season, for instance, began April 2 and closed July 21, but during that 109-day period, the club played 94 games, experienced 13 rainouts, logged 17,000 bus miles, and enjoyed just two off-days.

During this period, Judy and his Pittsburgh teammates often engaged their white counterparts in exhibition games. In 1934, the Grays faced Dizzy Dean's All-Stars 15 times. The black stars won nine.

The third baseman ended the drudgery of long road trips, poor food, second-rate accommodations, and occasional bigotry by retiring from baseball in 1936. For the next 16 years, he worked in a variety of jobs, ranging from a supervisor at Continental Can Company to driving a school bus.

In 1952, baseball welcomed Judy back. His long-time admirer, Connie Mack, hired Johnson as a scout and spring training coach for the Philadelphia Athletics.

The former Negro Leaguer quickly proved that he possessed a keen eye for talent. He recommended the A's sign Larry Doby, Minnie Minoso, and Henry Aaron. But due to lack of funds, Mack rejected all three. For less than $15,000, Philadelphia missed out on three young players who each would become superstars.

In 1956, the Milwaukee Braves tabbed Judy as an East Coast scout. An old friend, Handy Hayward, mentioned a young man he considered worth a look. Johnson watched the lightning-quick outfielder and filed a positive recommendation. The Braves agreed with their scout's evaluation and signed Bill Bruton. Bruton eventually inked another document with the Johnson household, a marriage license with Judy and Anita's daughter, Loretta.

Braves general manager John Quinn joined the Philadelphia Phillies in 1959 and brought Johnson into the scouting department. Judy's input played a major role in the Phil's acquisition of power- hitting Dick Allen. The ex-Negro League star remained on the Phillie's payroll until the early 1970s.

In 1989, the former player/manager of the Homestead Grays suffered a stroke. He died July 14, 1989, just three months short of his 90th birthday.

In his later years, Johnson reflected on his baseball past. "I always wished I had the chance to get to the big leagues," he recalled. "When we were playing against the major league stars, I would pray at night that I would have a good day against them. We had to prove we were the same quality as they were, and nine times out of ten we would."

On August 18, 1975, the National Baseball Hall of Fame and Museum inducted William "Judy" Johnson. The class of 1975 included Johnson, Earl Averill, Bucky Harris, Billy Herman, and Ralph Kiner.

Johnson's heart condition hindered his

acceptance speech. Overwhelmed with emotion, he struggled with his words.

"I never dreamed I would be remembered by the Hall of Fame," he said. "I want to thank all the people that made this possible. I thought I had been forgotten. Now I turn around and find myself on the same dais with such great stars as Stan Musial, Hank Greenberg, and Bob Feller."

Oscar Charleston

Oscar Charleston

It's impossible for anyone to be a better ball player than Oscar Charleston. — Sportswriter Grantland Rice

Born in 1896, Oscar Charleston lived the rough life of a poor son of a poor family in and around Indianapolis, Indiana. He managed to finish grammar school before circumstances forced him to leave home at age 15 to enlist in the peacetime U.S. Army.

In those days the army was segregated, and Charleston was placed in the all-black 24th Infantry Regiment, shortly to be shipped overseas. His unit maintained peace and order throughout the Philippine Islands, a protectorate acquired by the U.S. after the Spanish-American War. Despite dreary circumstances, the teenager and his fellow Americans found time to play baseball.

A natural athlete, Charleston ran track and played baseball for the regimental teams. A pioneer of sorts, the Indiana native even participated in the 1914 Manila Baseball League as their sole African-American representative.

After five years of arduous duty, the teenage soldier received his discharge and returned to Indianapolis. His tough upbringing combined with the rigors of military life had forged Charleston into the strongest of men.

C. I. Taylor, manager of the ABC's baseball squad, sought out the ex-soldier and offered him a contract for $50 a month. Sponsored by the American Brewing Company, the Indianapolis club fielded some of the country's best black baseball talent. Charleston teamed with second baseman Elwood "Bingo" DeMoss and outfielder Jimmy Lyons to create a formidable diamond trio.

Teammate Dave Malacher recalled meeting the soldier turned outfielder in 1916: "He was all muscle and bone, no fat, no stomach, perfect broad shoulders, fine strong legs, strong muscular arms, and powerful hands and fingers. He was fast, and he was strong."

The ABC's centerfielder also soon displayed another facet of his personality, his violent, temperamental nature. In an October 1916 exhibition game against a white all-star team, DeMoss argued a close play. Charleston rushed in and knocked the umpire to the ground. Fans charged the field, and the police barely prevented a full-scale riot. The authorities arrested DeMoss and Charleston but allowed them to post bail. The duo then skipped town to Cuba for the winter baseball season.

As his career moved forward in Cuba and the States, tales of the outfielder's great strength grew legendary. Some claimed the Indiana native could twist the horsehide cover off a baseball with his bare hands. On a road trip in Louisiana, Charleston flipped a roadster full of teammates into a ditch. The giant man wrenched the steering wheel off attempting to maintain control of the careening car. Here was a man whose physical presence intimidated even the bravest of men.

In 1919, Oscar moved to Chicago and joined Rube Foster's American Giants. Though he played well, Foster reluctantly parted with the massive outfielder the following year when the president of the Negro National League reassigned Charleston to Indianapolis to give the newly formed league greater parity.

The Army veteran spent the 1921 season with the St. Louis Giants and returned to Indianapolis for a final stay in 1922. Following his marriage to Jane

Blaylock in November 1922, the Giants relocated to Harrisburg, Pennsylvania, and Charleston took over as player-manager.

After four years in Harrisburg, the ex-infantryman switched to the Hilldales, a black club headquartered in the Philadelphia suburbs, in 1928 and 1929. This job ended when bankruptcy terminated the organized Negro Leagues in 1930. Cum Posey, owner of the independent Homestead Grays, rescued Charleston from the unemployment line by signing him to his club.

Posey's star-studded lineup of Satchel Paige, Judy Johnson, Josh Gibson, and Charleston ruled black baseball on the East Coast. Two years later, Gus Greenlee lured the future Hall of Famers to his Pittsburgh Crawfords. Greenlee added "Cool Papa" Bell to the mix, and the Crawfords emerged as the greatest team in the annals of Negro baseball.

Slowed by age and increased weight, Charleston shifted from centerfield to first base. In spite of his expanding girth, his batting reflexes remained cat-quick, and the towering player continued his assaults on opposing pitchers.

Even as he began to wind down his career and look forward to life after baseball, Charleston maintained his fierce demeanor. On a train trip through Florida, a hooded member of the Ku Klux

Klan confronted the towering ballplayer. Rather than back down, Oscar snatched the hood away and challenged the Klansman one-on-one. The unmasked bigot realized the danger and quickly retreated.

In 1937, virtually the entire Crawford squad jumped ship and aligned with President Rafael Trujillo's Dominican Republic National team. The following season, they returned to the mainland and reorganized as the Toledo Crawfords.

For the next decade, Charleston drifted in and out of the Negro Leagues. He seldom took the field or swung the bat, but confined his involvement to managing. During later years, the former outfielder and first baseman skippered the Philadelphia Stars. In the off-season during World War II, Charleston worked at the Philadelphia Quartermaster Depot.

After the war, Oscar scouted for Branch Rickey's Brown Dodgers. He returned to his roots and concluded his career as the manager of the Indianapolis Clowns, leading the team to the league title in 1954.

Later that year, Charleston suffered a stroke in his Philadelphia home. He died on October 5th, nine days short of his 58th birthday.

Oscar Charleston joined Bob Lemon, Robin Roberts, Fred Lindstrom, Carl Hubbard, and Roger Connors as members of the National Baseball Hall of Fame. The ceremony took place August 9, 1976.

John Henry "Pop" Lloyd

John Henry "Pop" Lloyd

"Who's the best baseball player of all-time? If you mean in organized baseball, my answer would be Babe Ruth; but if you mean in all baseball, organized or unorganized, the answer would have to be a colored man named John Henry Lloyd."
—September 1938 *Esquire* magazine article

In his youth, John Henry Lloyd endured a difficult family situation. His father died shortly after his birth in 1884. His mother remarried shortly afterward, and left the young boy in the care of his grandmother.

Like most 19th century black boys, the future Hall of Famer received little formal education. As a young man, the Paltaka, Florida, native took a job as a delivery boy and played baseball after work.

Seeking economic advancement, Lloyd worked as a porter for the Southern Express Company. In his spare time, the lanky teenager played with a weekend semi-pro baseball club, the Jacksonville

Old Receivers. It would be the first, but not the last team to pay for John Henry's services.

In 1905, encouraged by those who knew the game, the Floridian traveled to Georgia and landed a catching position for the Macon Acmes. Protective masks had not been invented, and Lloyd combated countless foul tips. *Chicago Defender* sports columnist Cary B. Lewis described one incident:

> In the third inning a foul tip pounced on his left lamp; the lid closed. He moistened his finger, rubbed the bruised member, and kept on. In the seventh inning, another foul pounced on his right lamp; it sought redress in darkness. Lloyd, like a good sport, exclaimed, "Gentlemen, I guess I'll have to quit, I can't see the ball."

To prevent these foul ball confrontations, the enterprising young man purchased and wore a wire wastepaper basket over his head. This move would start an equipment revolution.

The following winter, the catcher with the homemade mask returned to Florida and waited on tables to make ends meet. Yet ever as he served meals, Lloyd continued to hone his skills with the hotel baseball squad.

Encouraged by his Southern success, Lloyd traveled to Philadelphia in 1906. The former catcher switched to the infield and signed with the Cuban X-Giants. He backed up second baseman Charlie Grant, the player John McGraw had attempted to pass off as Native American Chief Tokohoma five years earlier.

In the first of many roster moves, the slick fielder jumped to Sol White's rival Philadelphia Giants in 1907. White, a former shortstop, onverted Lloyd from second base and taught him the position's intricacies.

For over two decades, the six-foot infielder bounced between the black teams of the east coast and the midwest. Lloyd explained: "Wherever the money was, that's where I was."

After three seasons as a Philadelphia Giant, he joined Rube Foster's Leland Giants in Chicago. Following a year in the Windy City, Lloyd returned to the black eastern leagues as player-manager for the New York Lincoln Giants.

The Lincoln brigade challenged teams of every color and vanquished virtually every one. In 1911, the Harlem club won 105 games and lost but 17.

Two years later, the team tallied 101 victories with only six defeats.

During his tenure, Lloyd and his charges engaged in several exhibitions against major eague teams. The black team emerged victorious over the New York Highlanders (later, renamed the Yankees), New York Giants, and Philadelphia Phillies. Twenty-two game winner and Hall of Fame pitcher Grover Cleveland Alexander fell victim to the black stars, 9-2.

Summer's end sent the Florida native to the Caribbean to play in the Cuban Winter Leagues. His superb fielding earned the shortstop the Spanish nickname "Cuchara," meaning scoop or shovel. Lloyd gained the title from the clouds of dust he generated by snaring grounders just above the dirt surface.

In November 1909, Lloyd showcased his talents against America's best white baseball talent. The Detroit Tigers journeyed to Cuba for a series of exhibitions against the Havana Reds.

American League batting champion Ty Cobb joined his teammates after three matches had been played. The "Georgia Peach" immediately attempted to run the bases with the same reckless abandon he displayed in the American League. But Lloyd and his fellow Cubans threw the Tiger outfielder

out three times on the basepaths. His failures
against the Cubans so upset Cobb that the the
volatile Southerner vowed never to set foot on a
baseball diamond against blacks again.

Lloyd and Rube Foster reunited in 1914. After
losing a home-and-home series to the Lincoln
Giants, the midwest manager enticed four New
York stars to streak westward. In addition to their
star shortstop, the east coast squad lost pitcher Joe
Williams, third baseman Billy Francis, and outfielder Jude Gans.

The American Giants' strict disciplinarian and
the easygoing infielder remained together until War
World I, when Lloyd took a job in the United
States Army Quartermaster's depot in January
1918. When he refused to go south for the winter
league season, Foster replaced Lloyd with Bobby
Williams.

Undaunted by his dismissal or the onslaught of
time, the slick-fielding power hitter returned to his
Eastern roots. At age 34 and a step slower, he
shifted from shortstop to first base. For the next
dozen seasons, Lloyd played and managed for the
Brooklyn Royal Giants, the Columbus Buckeyes,
the Bacharach Giants of Atlantic City, the Hilldale
Club of Philadelphia, and the New York Lincoln
Giants.

Third baseman George Scales of the Lincoln Giants remembers Lloyd's consistent hitting: "When I first met Lloyd, he was an old man. He was a line drive hitter, a big ol' hitter who just laid on the ball. The older he got, the better he knew how to play. You'd think he was still a young man."

The soft-spoken, mild-mannered, fierce competitor never seemed to age. Even after Lloyd retired as an active Negro League player at age 48, he took the field for another 10 years in the Atlantic City semi-pro leagues.

Lloyd's managerial style differed from many of his contemporaries. Most bosses of that era emulated John McGraw and Connie Mack as rigid, no-nonsense field generals. But the ex-shortstop preferred to build his men up rather than tear them down. Hall of Fame third baseman Judy Johnson described his method with the 1923 Hilldale club: "He was a great man and a great teacher. He put the confidence in you, and you had to do it — you just had to do it."

John Henry Lloyd and his wife, Nan, had no children. But hundreds of young ballplayers received instruction from the Hall of Fame shortstop. He was so revered as a father figure that those Lloyd reared on the diamond nicknamed him "Pop."

After retiring from the Negro Leagues, Lloyd joined the Atlantic City, New Jersey, school system as a janitor. In addition to his custodial duties at the Indiana Avenue School, he served as the city's Little League commissioner. Nothing thrilled the former Negro Leaguer more than teaching others the game he loved. Whitey Gruhler, *Atlantic City Press* sports editor, described a scene played out on countless occasions:

> The youngsters cluster about him between sessions. They call him "Pop" and love to listen while he spins baseball yarns of the past. Sometimes they refuse to break away from him and "Pop" has to pick them up bodily and carry them into their classrooms. He is their hero, this big, soft-hearted, soft-spoken, congenial man with a tired look in his eyes, but the bubbling spirit of youth in his heart.

The Boardwalk City honored its adopted son and Little League commissioner in 1949 by naming a $150,000 recreational facility John Henry Lloyd Stadium. When asked during the ceremonies if he regretted his playing days concluded before baseball's color barrier fell, Lloyd replied in his typically genteel manner:

"I do not consider that I was born at the wrong time. I felt it was the right time, for I had the chance to prove the ability of our race in this sport, and because many of us did our very best to uphold the traditions of the game and of the orld of sport, we have given the Negro a greater opportunity now to be accepted into the major leagues with other Americans."

The man Honus Wagner said was baseball's best, died of arteriosclerosis in 1965 at the age of 80.

John Henry "Pop" Lloyd was inducted into the National Baseball Hall of Fame and Museum on August 8, 1977. Fellow inductees included Ernie Banks, Al Lopez, Joe Sewell, Martin Dihigo, and Amos Rusie. The Hall of Fame's Special Com- . mittee on the Negro Leagues disbanded soon afterward.

Andrew "Rube" Foster

Andrew "Rube" Foster

"We are the ship — All else the sea"
— Motto of the Negro National League

Andrew "Rube" Foster embraced Chicago's broad
shoulders with great passion. The city responded
with equal enthusiasm. The bond between the 6'4",
200-pound son of a black minister and the heartland
of the Midwest grew stronger each year.

For a decade Foster and his American Giants
provided Chicago's citizens with the finest baseball
in the country. More important than his play on the
field, it was Rube's behind-the-scenes work as team
owner and league executive that dramatically
changed African-American baseball.

Foster's long journey to the Windy City began
September 17, 1879 in the small town of Calvert,
Texas, where Andrew's father pastored the African
Methodist Episcopal Church. As a child, Andrew
suffered from respiratory ailments. The local doctor
advised his parents to keep the youngster out-of-

doors as much as possible. In those long hours in the sun, Foster developed a love for hitting a ball with a stick.

Andrew's mother died as the boy entered his teens. His father eventually moved to Victoria, in southeastern Texas, leaving the young man at loose ends.

Since black sharecroppers in the Brazos River Valley fared little better than slaves, Foster left Calvert to seek his fortune. The 13-year-old boy traveled across the Lone Star State, hooking up with several touring semi-pro baseball teams.

Riding the rails and playing for meager money toughened the youth and taught lessons no school could provide. Foster recalled those days as "bitter, heart-breaking memories."

At this time, many considered baseball "low and ungentlemanly," so fellow blacks often shunned him. In the face of growing criticism of his choice of occupations, the six-foot, four-inch righthander developed as the top amateur pitcher in Texas.

Playing for the Waco Yellow Jackets and the Fort Worth Colts, the Calvert native hurled countless games while travelling across Texas and its bordering states. In 1901, Foster even journeyed to Hot Springs, Arkansas, and pitched batting practice against Connie Mack's Philadelphia Athletics.

Not long after this display against major league talent, the tall righthander caught the eye of Frank Leland. The veteran club owner needed fresh arms to challenge the supremacy of Chicago's number one semi-pro team, the Unions.

He offered Foster a contract, and Rube joined the Leland Giants with great enthusiasm. He boasted, "It will be a case of Greek meeting Greek. I fear nobody." But the unsophisticated Texan pitched erratically with Leland's organization. At mid-season he bolted the Giants and joined a white squad in Otsego, Michigan.

The rough edges smoothed as Foster quickly matured. He developed a deadly screwball, thrown with an underhand delivery. The next year, Rube headed east and joined the staff of the Cuban X-Giants, a black touring team loosely based in New York.

Legends and lore surrounded the fierce fire-baller. Although no newspaper account or boxscore exists for verification, it is thought Foster outdueled future Philadelphia Athletic Hall of Famer George "Rube" Waddell in a Sunday afternoon exhibition. Whether fact or fiction, the tale earned Foster the nickname "Rube." He readily accepted the label and answered to it for the rest of his life.

Another mythical figure entered the life of the black hurler during this period. Some claim New York Giant manager John McGraw engaged Foster to teach Christy Mathewson, John "Iron Man" McGinnity, and Leon "Red" Ames his screwball. Although this incident may be glorified fable, McGraw and Foster maintained a relationship for many years.

Philadelphia witnessed Foster's pitching prowess for four years. After a season of hurling for E. B. Lamar's X-Giants, the ace, accompanied by virtually the entire team , jumped to the opposition, the Philadelphia Giants, in 1904.

When the two powerhouses squared off in the 1904 "Colored Championship of the World," Rube struck out 18 batters in an 8-4 opening victory. The X-Giants evened the series in game two, but Foster hurled a two-hitter in game three, winning 4-2, and capturing the championship for the Philadelphia Giants.

Rube reached the pinnacle of his career in 1905. Black baseball historian Norman "Tweed" Webb has credited the righthander with 51 wins and only five losses. Pittsburgh Pirate Hall of Fame shortstop Honus Wagner described Foster as "the smoothest pitcher I've ever seen."

Like today's free agent ballplayers, the hard-throwing pitcher forsook Philadelphia for a bigger paycheck. He returned to Chicago and rejoined Frank Leland's Giants as player-manager, taking eight teammates with him.

Under Foster's command, the Leland Giants dominated the almost all-white Chicago city leagues from 1907 to 1910. In their first year, the country's best semi-pro team won 110 games, including 48 in a row. They lost only 10.

Many rate the 1910 team as Chicago's all-time best. Led by Hall of Fame shortstop John Henry "Pop" Lloyd, catcher Bruce Petway, a pitching staff of Foster, Pat Dougherty, and Frank Wickware, the pride of the Midwest claimed 123 victories and a mere six losses.

The star pitcher and manager wrested control from Frank Leland in 1910. The split enabled Foster to partner with John Schorling, a son-in-law of Chicago White Sox owner Charles Comiskey. The duo renamed the team the American Giants, and Schorling purchased the former Sox ballpark located at 39th and Shields streets.

Comiskey predicted failure for the black team if their schedule conflicted with Chicago's major league teams. Foster scoffed at the notion and challenged the Cubs and the Sox for the fans' affection.

The masses responded and proved the black entrepreneur correct. One Sunday afternoon in 1911, the Cubs drew 6,000, the White Sox 9,000, and the American Giants topped the turnstile count with 11,000.

As the years passed, Foster pitched less and less. By 1915, his role shifted to manager except for occasional special attractions and promotions. Often he signaled plays by puffing on his pipe. The one-time ace of black baseball remained a brilliant showman. Thousands attended the contests to watch Foster and his intricate moves.

Floyd "Jelly" Gardner, an American Giant outfielder, recalled: "One day he'd take his pipe out of his mouth for a steal or motion this way with his hand. Most of the time he'd give signs with his head, like he'd be talking with some people and he'd nod his head a certain way and that would be a sign. Sometimes he'd give signs by puffing on his pipe — a couple of puffs might mean steal."

The American Giants built their strategy around speed and daring. In addition to strong pitching and slick defense, Foster advocated bunting and stealing and expected his players to be adept at both. The field general perfected the unconventional hit-and-run bunt. The play entailed a runner on first base breaking with the pitch and continuing to third while the fielder threw out the batter.

The Giants' reputation stretched from coast to coast. They wintered in Cuba or Florida, playing exhibitions against local squads. In the spring, the team journeyed throughout the South and West, engaging both semi-pros and minor leaguers along the way.

Foster brought style and grace to the organization. The American Giants traveled in private Pullman cars, wore the classiest uniforms, and used the best equipment.

Dave Malarcher, former Chicago third baseman, recalled the first time he encountered the American Giants in New Orleans, "I never saw such a well-equipped ball club in my whole life! Every day they came out in a different set of beautiful uniforms, all kinds of balls and bats, all the best kinds of equipment."

As the 1920s approached, however, the City with the Broad Shoulders began to change. Nonblack veterans returning from World War I discovered the Windy City's black population had doubled, from mass migration of poor sharecroppers from the South, between 1916 to 1919. Jobs had been lost, and blacks had moved into formally white areas.

Southside white "athletic clubs" raided black neighborhoods. Blacks retaliated. The infamous Chicago race riot occurred on July 27, 1919, at the 29th Street beach. The city's morale deteriorated further when rumors of a "fix" in the 1919 World Series by the Chicago White Sox (soon to be dubbed "The Black Sox") circulated freely. Public faith and confidence weakened.

In the face of turmoil and doubt, the resourceful Foster kept pace with the changing times. In the winter of 1920, the diamond genius fulfilled his lifelong dream, uniting black baseball under a single umbrella; he convinced the owners of the best black teams in the Midwest to band together as the Negro National League.

It was this organization would pave the way for future black athletes Jackie Robinson, Larry Doby, Monte Irvin, Willie Mays, and Henry Aaron to break a racial barrier existing since the 1880's.

On February 13, 1920, representatives met in the Kansas City YMCA to establish the new organization. They drew up a constitution barring raids on member teams, instituted a reserve clause binding players to their teams, and provided fines for inappropriate behavior on and off the field. An eight-team league emerged, consisting of Foster's American Giants, the Indianapolis ABCs, the Detroit Stars, the St. Louis Stars, the Chicago Giants, the Cuban Giants, the Dayton Marcos, and the Kansas City Monarchs. The organization selected the motto, "We are the ship — All else the sea."

Foster captained the ship with a stern but fair hand. He shuffled players between teams for competitive balance. He advanced funds to struggling franchises. He loaned money to needy players.

Even though he always seemed to act in the best interests of the league, the combined roles of president and treasurer of the Negro National League, owner and manager of the Chicago American Giants, and general manager of two other clubs eventually led to conflicts of interest. Under pressure, Foster resigned as league president in 1925.

In 1926, Foster met with baseball's white power brokers, Ban Johnson and John McGraw. Although no one knows for certain the details of this meeting, rumors persisted that the Negro League president proposed adding all-black teams to play in the

American and National Leagues. But the proposal went nowhere.

Perhaps disillusioned by his inability to break the color line, Rube kept pushing himself to expand black baseball. The pressure from long hours and hard work eventually caused Foster to collapse mentally. His family was forced to admit him to the state hospital in Kankakee, Illinois.

The former pitcher, manager, and league president never returned to normal life. He died December 9, 1930, at age 51.

Floral bouquets by the dozens adorned St. Mark's African Methodist Episcopal Church for Foster's funeral. Three thousand mourners packed the sanctuary for the service. Thousands more waited patiently in the cold December rain to view the man who brought Chicago the finest baseball in the country. All wept as the choir sang, "Rock of Ages."

The rock of the Negro National League envisioned a world where blacks and whites would compete equally on the field of play. Unfortunately, he died before his dream became reality. Yet Andrew "Rube" Foster's dream never died. His vision and foresight paved the way for other African-American ballplayers.

The National Baseball Hall of Fame and Museum's Veteran Committee elected Andrew "Rube" Foster in 1981. He became the first black baseball star to receive induction since the disbandment of the Negro League Committee in 1977.

Bob Gibson and Johnny Mize joined Foster as honorees in the August 2nd ceremony. Earl Foster, Rube's 71-year-old son, accepted his award.

"I never heard him say anything when I was young," Earl said. "The only thing I knew was that a few men in baseball said they would let my father's team into baseball but not all the others. They died a few years later, so it never happened."

Ray "Dandy" Dandridge

Ray "Dandy" Dandridge

"When they were talking about bringing Jackie Robinson to the major leagues, a lot of people thought they should have brought up Ray Dandridge instead. That tells a lot about how he was. He's the best third baseman I ever saw in my life." — Former Dodger manager Tommy Lasorda.

Ray Dandridge was born August 13, 1913, in Richmond, Virginia. The black youngster moved with his family to Buffalo, New York, at age 10. Attending integrated schools, he played whatever sport was in season: football, basketball, boxing, and of course, baseball. In the ninth grade, Dandridge dropped out of school and concentrated solely on the diamond sport, playing for local teams.

At age 18, the youth returned to Richmond and played semi-pro ball. In the sandlot leagues, he competed against two athletes, Buck Leonard and Dave Barnhill, who would become his future black baseball colleagues. Ray learned and grew, hungrily searching for the next window of opportunity.

In 1933, the Detroit Stars barnstormed through Virginia. Manager Candy Jim Taylor took note of the strapping young man on the opposing team and the massive home run he slugged in their exhibition game against the local nine. Dandridge refused the Stars' first offer, but Taylor wouldn't accept no for an answer. He directed the team bus to the young man's house.

Ray's father surprised him. Confined to a wheelchair because of a mill accident, Archie Dandridge encouraged his son to give professional baseball a try. The 19-year-old dodged the issue. He left the house and walked to the local pool hall. After several hours, he returned home and made sure no barnstormers remained.

Early the next morning, Taylor reappeared with the offer. Archie insisted Ray pack his bags and head out with the team, and the young man finally agreed.

Later, Dandy learned why the elder Dandridge had been so persuasive. "They bribed my father with $25. But right now, I'm kind of glad my father did encourage me to go. I appreciate my daddy telling me to go out and take a chance in the world."

Taylor took the youngster to the batting cage.

He forced Dandridge to exchange his lightweight bat for a heavier model. The manager instructed his player in the art of hitting to all fields. He punched outside pitches to right, pulled inside ones to left, and stroked ones over the plate straight through the middle. The Richmond native absorbed the lesson well and batted over .300 the rest of his career.

Like most professional black baseball teams of the early 1930's, the Detroit Stars struggled to turn a profit. By summer's end, the Stars had folded, and Dandridge returned to Richmond with nothing but a little experience.

The following spring, Dick Lundy, player-manager for the Newark Dodgers, asked the teenager to give professional baseball another try. Lundy moved him to third base, and Dandridge played the position as if it had been ordained. Former Negro Leaguers observed, "You could drive a train through his legs but not a baseball." His teammates nicknamed Dandridge "Dandy" for his slick fielding. Opponents showed little mercy, calling him "Squatty" or "Hooks."

In 1935, Ray's second year as Dodger, the 21-year-old earned his first of three trips to the Negro East-West All-Star game. The infielder played four seasons in Newark and teamed with Willie Wells to create the best third base-shortstop combination in the Negro Leagues.

In 1940, owner Jorge Pasquel lured Dandridge to the Mexican League with a $10,000 salary. The slick fielder greatly enjoyed the money, the easy-going lifestyle, and the respect he received south of the border before he returned to Newark for two seasons. Dandridge played with the Veracruz Diablos until 1943, and Mexico beckoned again after the war.

In 1948, Pasquel died tragically in a plane crash. His death killed the hopes and dreams of turning the Mexican League into a third major league. With Pasquel's death, most transplanted Americans drifted back to the states.

The New York Cubans hired Ray as their player-manager. A year later, Dandridge received the break of a lifetime when the New York Giants purchased his contract as well as that of teammate Dave Barnhill.

The Negro League stars caught the first available train to the Big Apple. They had scarcely stepped off the platform when the front office headquartered in the Polo Grounds delivered startling news; the duo must report to the organization's top minor league team, the Minneapolis Millers, immediately. Dandridge bade his family in Newark a quick farewell and boarded an airplane for the Land of 10,000 Lakes.

General manager Rosy Ryan met the pair at the airport and took them straight to Nicollet Park. Dandy and Barnhill arrived in the bottom of the eighth inning of the first game of a Sunday afternoon doubleheader. It surprised everyone when Manager Tommy Heath immediately inserted his newly acquired infielder. Dandridge confidently strode to the plate. Ray was immediately "welcomed" by opposing pitcher Mickey McDermott who dusted him with a fastball only inches from his ear. Not intimidated, Dandridge sent the second pitch screaming through the middle for a solid single.

In game two, the infielder starred with his glove, covering more territory than anyone could imagine. Former major league pitcher Hoyt Wilhelm recalled, "No matter where the ball was hit, he always made the throw so that he just did get the man at first." Ray had spent his whole life preparing for this moment, and he wasn't going to blow it.

Yet the major league Giants would fail to capitalize on their astute acquisition. The Minneapolis Millers received the benefit. In 1949, Ray hit .362, missing the batting title by a scant two points. The next year, he led the American Association in hits (195), at bats (627), and batting average (.311). The League awarded the 37-year-old infielder the Most Valuable Player award.

Despite his success at the minor's highest level, the Giants never added Dandridge to their big league roster. He thrilled Minnesota fans for two more seasons but never got a ticket to the "Bigs."

The Phillies and Athletics attempted a trade, but the Giants refused. Since organized baseball allowed a player only four years on a single minor league team roster, New York sold Dandridge's contract to the Sacremento in 1953. He finished the year with the Oakland Oaks.

Ray spent a final season with Bismarck at age 42 in 1955. As the season wound down, Dandridge knew his playing days had ended too.

Former teammate and fellow Negro Leaguer Roy Campanella summed his career best. "There has never been a third baseman who could play better than Dandridge. I don't care who it was—Brooks Robinson, Graig Nettles, Pie Traynor — nobody."

Retiring from the game he loved, the long-time ballplayer returned to his adopted home of Newark. Dandridge worked as the supervisor of a recreation center before retiring to Florida in 1984. He died of cancer on February 12, 1994.

The Veterans Committee selected another Negro Leaguer to the National Baseball Hall of Fame and Museum in 1987. Ray "Dandy" Dandridge joined Jim "Catfish" Hunter and Billy Williams in the July 27 induction ceremonies.

The long-overdue recognition brought the black baseball star a sense of appreciation and relief. "Thank you, each and every one of the Veterans Committee," he said. "Thank you for allowing me to smell the roses."

"If I had to do it all over again," Dandridge concluded, "I think I'd do it the same way. I love the game of baseball, and it looked like today baseball loved me."

Leon Day

Leon Day

"No one ever got too many runs off Leon Day. He was a great pitcher, simply great. He had the heart of a lion and was so valuable to the team because he also could play second or center field."— Hall of Fame outfielder Monte Irvin.

The massive GI crowd cheered as Leon Day took the mound. Over 100,000 soldiers packed the Nuremberg stadium to witness the Overseas Invasion Service Expedition (OISE) team take on General George S. Patton's Third Army nine. In the same arena where Adolf Hitler had inspired Germany's masses, these Americans found a time and place for baseball only a few months after the end of World War II.

With bullet-ridden battlefields still vividly etched in their memories, military personnel gathered in postwar peacetime to celebrate the national pastime. Patton, a four-star general, demanded the best in everything and packed his squad with former major leaguers. Ewell "The

Whip" Blackwell and Ken Heintzelman anchored the pitching staff. Harry "The Hat" Walker, Johnny Wyrostek, and Benny Zientara provided solid hitting and defense.

Day and fellow Negro Leaguer Willard Brown led the OISE contingent in experience. The rest had never ventured beyond the sandlots. At best, the OISE team could be classified as "semi-pro."

When the units tangled on the diamond, however, heart and desire prevailed over experience. Day took a 2-1 lead into the bottom of the ninth.

The first batter led off with a triple. Walker, Wyrostek, and Zientara waited. "I pitched Walker high and tight," Day remembered. "With all left-handers, I always went high and tight."

Walker struck out, and the drama built. With the crowd roaring, the left-handed Wyrostek swung and missed at three pitches, all high and tight. Finally with thousand creating a deafening roar, Zientara also went down swinging. With little display of emotion, Day adjusted his cap humbly and walked away the victor with a nifty four-hitter.

The professional ballplayers on loan to the United States Army wondered. Who was this Day? Where did he come from? How did he learn to pitch so well? How could a black man show us up?

For this first time in his life, the Negro pitcher felt like an equal. On foreign soil, he could challenge his white counterparts on even terms. "I was bearing down on them," he explained. "I never had any trouble with the major leaguers I faced in Europe." And he could win too.

The Negro League pitcher later engaged Blackwell in an exhibition in Nice, France. Brown backed up his hurler with two home runs, and Day coasted to an 8-0 shutout.

* * *

Thirty years before displaying his major league talent in the armed forces, Leon Day had been born on October 30, 1916 in Alexandria, Virginia. While he was just a baby, his family moved to Mount Winans, Maryland, where the black boy grew up in the shadows of Westport Park, home of the Baltimore Black Sox.

Every Sunday, Leon trekked to the ballpark. He recalled, "It was within walking distance, but it was a good walk, about two miles. I'd go over the fence, under the fence, or sometimes I'd get a foul ball, and they'd let me in."

At age twelve, Day joined the Mount Winans Athletic Club sandlot team. Several years later, he earned the second base slot with a semi-pro team, the Silver Moons. As the season waned, Mac Eggleston, catcher and manager for the pick-up club, contacted Rap Dixon, player-manager of the Black Sox. Day impressed the skipper and joined the black ballclub for spring training in 1934.

The Black Sox struggled between the lines with their combination of aging veterans and inexperienced youngsters. Dixon promised the 17-year-old $60 per month, but often he reneged and parceled out only a dollar or two. Disenchanted with the unfulfilled promise, Day searched for a way out.

Buck Leonard, the Homestead Gray all-star first baseman, watched the teenage pitcher and attempted to lure him away with a $125 monthly salary. Dixon learned of Day's exit plans and thwarted them by marching his hurler back to his hotel room and practically holding him hostage. It would take almost a year for him to escape.

Persistent pleading persuaded Leon's father to let him give baseball another try the following season. The elder Day grudgingly agreed, and Leon switched from the Black Sox to the Brooklyn Eagles.

During spring training, Eagles' manager Candy Jim Taylor called on the teenager to pitch batting practice. The untutored youth threw without a windup and cocked the ball behind his ear. Though his three-quarters overhand delivery looked unconventional, his pitches seldom missed the strike zone and his fastball blazed past hitters. Coupled with a dandy curveball and good changeup, Day was christened, "Ace of the Eagles."

The young hurler's mastery over batters earned him the first of six appearances on the East-West Negro League All- Star team. The annual contest in Chicago drew thousands of black fans and often surpassed the attendance of the Negro World Series. He impressed them all.

The following season, Abe and Effa Manley purchased the Brooklyn Eagles and Newark Dodgers franchises and combined them. The newly-named Newark Eagles backed Day with a "Million Dollar Infield." Future Hall of Famers Ray Danridge and Willie "The Devil" Wells manned third and short. Mule Suttles and Dick Seay held down first and second. It was an incredible combination.

Newark challenged the Homestead Grays for Negro League supremacy in 1936 and 1937.

The Eagles would struggle, however, in 1938, losing Day for the season with a shoulder injury. Like most of his black colleagues, the pitcher had journeyed to Latin America for the winter campaign. Day slipped in the Cuban Almendares' locker room and felt something pop. It would cost him a full season. Without benefit of a therapist, Day worked the arm into shape. He lifted irons to rebuild its strength and threw endlessly until the soreness went away.

The all-star rejoined the Eagles in 1939 and 1940, but the Grays still reigned supreme. Lured by a bigger paycheck, Day and Willie Wells switched to the Mexican League in 1940.

The two mended their fences with the Eagles and returned for the '41, '42 and '43 campaigns. Just prior to the 1942 East-West All-Star Game, Day struck out 18 Baltimore Elite Giants and allowed only one hit, a bloop single, during the game. The fireballer put baseball on hold, however, when Uncle Sam drafted him for the army in September of 1943.

Nine months later, the pitcher dodged flying bullets and raining artillery shells delivering ammunition and supplies to the troops on Normandy's beaches. "I remember one night when I came out of the water with a load of ammunition," Day recalled. "I heard the planes coming, so I jumped out of the truck and ran up the bank. The planes strafed everything and shot up the entire beach." He was lucky to have survived.

Shortly after the post-war exhibition series in Europe, the Negro Leaguer returned to the United States. During the 1946 season, Day manned the mound for the Eagles' opener against the Philadelphia Stars.

The former GI was on top of his game. The Stars collected no hits, and only two reached first base. Day walked one batter, and another reached on an error by shortstop Benny Fielder. Newark handed the six-time all-star a 2-0 Opening Day victory.

Unknown to the thousands who watched his comeback, Day suffered an arm injury during the contest. It would eventually force him from baseball. Pitching through pain, the gritty trooper never complained, helping lead the Eagles to the Negro National League title. Newark then defeated the Kansas City Monarchs in the Black World Series to reign as the Negro League champion.

Day never returned to the Eagles. Ex-teammate Willie Wells convinced him to go south once more, and the ace of Newark pitched in 1947 and 1948 for the Mexican League.

The United States beckoned for the last time. Day signed with the Baltimore Elite Giants in '49, but black baseball faced a lingering death. The best players had switched to the Dodgers, Giants, and

Indians. With a weak arm and advancing age, Day now had no hope of pitching in the majors. Still ,he kept coming back for one curtain call after another. The Negro Leaguer wore the uniform another five years. He pitched in several Canadian leagues until 1955 before retiring permanently from the game he so loved.

Day returned to his roots in Baltimore and worked as a bartender and a security guard. The former Eagle never complained that the country that asked him to fight for freedom in war never gave him the chance to pitch in the major leagues in peace time.

The National Baseball Hall of Fame elected Leon Day to membership on March 7, 1995. Six days later, he died of heart failure at age 78.

On July 30, 1995, the Hall of Fame held posthumous induction ceremonies for Leon Day. His fellow honorees included Mike Schmidt, Richie Asburn, Vic Willis, and William Hulbert.

Day's widow, Geraldine, accepted his award. Mrs. Day implored for the admission of additional ex-Negro League players. "I pray one day it will be made right," she said.

Willie "Bill" Foster

Willie "Bill" Foster

"Bill Foster was my star pitcher, the greatest pitcher of our time not even barring Satchel Paige."—Former Chicago American Giant manager Dave Malarcher

Willie Foster's pathway from childhood to pitching ace was rocky. He was the much-younger brother of "Rube" Foster, a rising star in black baseball, but the family was not particularly close. The father had lost his first wife, Rube's mother, and then remarried Jennie Stuart. The Methodist minister would die himself shortly after Willie's birth on June 14, 1904.

Jennie Stuart Foster moved her young son to Rodney, Mississippi, to be closer to her family. But death visited once more and claimed the widow Foster when Willie was only four. The responsibility of raising the boy fell to his maternal grandparents.

All through childhood, young Foster heard tales

of his famous half-brother. With each passing year, he desired more and more to join the great Rube Foster and his legendary Chicago American Giants. Though education greatly expanded his mind, it couldn't quench Willie's passion for baseball. When he got a chance, he returned to his first love.

It was here that fate finally smiled on the black youngster. His grandparents enrolled him in Alcorn College's laboratory school. The education Willie received far exceeded that of most black or white children in the early 20th century.

The 15-year-old, six-foot, two-inch lefthanded pitcher longed to play professional baseball. He made the journey to Chicago and sought out his prodigal half-brother, Rube, the owner-manager-pitcher of the American Giants.

He expected encouragement. Instead, he received rejection. Rube told Bill to return to Rodney, Mississippi, and complete his education at Alcorn College. The youngster dutifully complied, but resentment boiled inside.

Even as Foster enrolled in school, he continued playing baseball. Every summer, he pitched for the local Rodney nine. Over time, his body matured, and his skills improved.

By 1924, professional teams clamored for his services. The young man from Mississippi initially

signed with the Memphis Red Sox. Several months
later, Rube discovered his relative pitching for the
competition. As president of the Negro National
League, he ordered the Memphis ownership to
assign Bill to the American Giants.

The younger Foster recalled, "Naturally, it was a
sore spot between my brother and me for a long
time. I told Rube, 'Why didn't you take me before I
went up to Memphis?' I never did get over that. I
decided from then on I was going to do everything
like I wanted to do it. He would try to show me the
right way, and I didn't know the right way nor the
wrong way. I didn't know anything. But I was just
going to be obstinate, you know."

Bill struggled while he ignored his half-brother's
coaching and advice. In 1926, however, Rube
suffered a nervous breakdown and entered the
Illinois State Mental Hospital. Moved by the
tragedy, Willie's heart softened. He practiced the
techniques Rube preached and took his pitching
tips to heart.

The turnaround amazed everyone. Bill went
from mediocrity to stardom almost overnight. In
1926, the lefthander won 29 games and lost only
three. The next year, he improved to 32 and 3.

From 1926 to 1937, Bill dominated Negro
League pitching. Unofficially, he won 137 games

and lost only 62, ranking as black baseball's all-time percentage victory leader. The hard-throwing lefthander notched 26 wins in a row in 1926.

Foster led the American Giants to back-to-back championships in 1926 and 1927 and again in 1932 and 1933. Unlike most Negro Leaguers, Bill spent virtually his entire career in Chicago. Except for brief stints with the Homestead Grays and Kansas City Monarchs in 1931, Foster wore only the colors of the American Giants.

The overpowering lefty hurled a complete game in the inaugural Black East-West All-Star game in 1933. His West squad defeated the East, 11-7.

Throught the years, fans flocked by the thousands to watch Foster battle fellow Hall-of-Famer Satchel Paige. In 27 head-to-head matchups, the lefthanded pitcher bested the better-known Paige, 14-13. Foster's 137 official career Negro League victories edged Satchel by eight for the greatest number in black baseball history.

As a young pitcher, the lefty relied on a blazing fastball. When he matured, Foster's curve rivaled that of any major league ballplayer.

Former Kansas City Monarch pitcher Hilton Smith recalled, "Foster had two curveballs. He'd throw one high — that's the one he wanted to get called a strike. Then when he got ready for you to swing, he'd start it around you waist, and the catcher would catch in the dirt. You couldn't hit it with anything."

His American Giant manager, Dave Malarcher echoed Smith's sentiments. "Willie Foster's greatness was that he had this terrific speed and great, fast-breaking curveball and a drop ball, and he was really a master of the change-of-pace. He could throw you a real fast one and then use the same motion and bring it up a little slower, and then a little slower yet. And then he'd use the same motion again, and Z-zzzz! He was really a great pitcher."

Bill pitched for several semi-pro teams in 1938 before retiring from the game. He entered the insurance business in his adopted state of Mississippi and later managed the Harlem Globetrotters for Abe Saperstein.

In 1960, his alma mater, Alcorn State, hired him as their baseball coach. He later became Dean of Men and retired from the school in 1977.

Bill Foster died September 16, 1978. The National Baseball Hall of Fame enshrined him posthumously in 1996. Willie and Rube Foster joined the Waners, Paul and Lloyd, and the Wrights, George and

Harry, as the only brother combinations so honored.

Willie "Bill" Foster was honored by the National Baseball Hall of Fame and Museum on August 4, 1996. Earl Weaver, Jim Bunning, and Ned Hanlon also comprised the class of 1996.

Foster's son, Bill, Jr., represented his father. His brief remarks rang with emotion and poignancy. "Dad, you made it," he said.

Willie "The Devil" Wells

Willie "The Devil" Wells

"The finest shortstop, black or white." — Newark
Eagles owner Effa Manley

Willie Wells was born in Austin, Texas, on
October 10, 1905. Growing up, he seldom saw his
pullman porter father, but Willie and his mother
bonded closely.

Cisco Wells believed in education, not "foolish"
games. However, her son thought otherwise. As he
moved from boyhood to teen age, he spent every
free moment at Dobbs Field and became friendly
with Biz Mackey, a catcher from nearby San
Marcos. The duo later would become teammates
with the Newark Eagles.

Willie loved baseball. And he knew well the
marginal employment prospects of a black man in
the Lone Star State. Who could ask for a better life
than to be paid for playing a boy's game?

Cisco Wells had her own ideas. She convinced
Wille that a degree from Sam Huston College

would pave the path to success. But a telegram to Willie from the Philadelphia Royals offered the princely sum of $400 to play baseball. Shortstop Bill Riggins had broken a leg in the California winter leagues. The Royals needed an immediate replacement and had sought out the youthful Texan.

Wells decided to forego college and cast his fortunes with baseball. Without asking his mother's approval, the teenager headed for the West Coast.

"I got my clothes and slipped away," he recalled. "I had never seen California, and I wanted to see it. I told them to send my mother the money and just give me expenses."

Willie knew the venture was a risk. The previous summer the teenager had experienced mixed results with the St. Louis Stars. Veterans shunned him and pulled cruel practical jokes. Curveballs baffled him, and the Gateway to the West seemed light years away from Austin, Texas.

Unlike St. Louis, the California trip worked wonders. The Royals manager treated Willie like a son. Hurley McNair, an outfielder with the Kansas City Monarchs, also took the young Texan under his wing. He saw Wells' struggle with the curve and sought a remedy.

McNair tied Willie's foot to home plate with a piece of rope to prevent the infielder from stepping away. The outfielder pitched batting practice for hours and fed the youngster a steady diet of breaking pitches. After hours and hours of hitting, the Texan mastered a pitcher's great equalizer.

When Wells returned for spring training, hurlers eagerly awaited his time at bat. Remembering his weakness, the shortstop saw nothing but curveballs. But now Willie was prepared. "Every time they'd break a curveball," he recalled, "I'd hit it on a line somewhere, up against the fence or between the fielders." Installed as the starting shortstop, the now confident sophomore fielded smoothly and hit .379, the second highest batting average in the league.

In the spring of 1925, Rube Foster's Chicago American Giants and the St. Louis Stars trained in Texas. Both teams observed the slick fielder and maneuvered to sign him.

Willie's mother refused their offers at first, but her son persisted. Finally, she relented, but only if the teenager signed with St. Louis, an overnight train ride from Austin. Wells quickly grew close to his teammates, especially James "Cool Papa" Bell. Many evenings the two country boys remained in their rooms and played cards rather than savor the St. Louis nightlife. Bell eventually married Willie's ex-girlfriend, and the trio formed a lifetime friendship.

During the late 1920s, St. Louis rose to the top of the Negro National League, winning three pennants in four years. Then hard times and a depression hit the League in the '30s, and the Stars fell into bankruptcy. Wells joined the Detroit Wolves, but like the Stars the team soon disbanded. Most of the Detroit squad hooked up with Pittsburgh's Homestead Grays, but Willie was disenchanted with the arduous travel demanded by Negro team owners.

"We'd play in Pittsburgh on Friday, Toronto on Saturday, then Detroit on Sunday," the shortstop remembered. "I finally said no more. I just want my health and I want to live."

Because of an easier travel schedule, the native Texan signed with his old rival, the Kansas City Monarchs. Former St. Louis players "Cool Papa" Bell and George Giles inked with the Kansas City nine as well, but Willie didn't remain in the Show Me state long.

A year later, Chicago American Giant owner Robert Cole convinced Wells to play in the Windy City. Ex-Stars Mule Suttles and Ted Trent joined him. Willie Foster, half-brother of former owner Rube Foster, Turkey Stearnes, and Alex Radcliffe combined with the former St. Louis standouts to capture the 1933 Negro National League flag.

Wells remained in Chicago until 1936 when financial problems arose once more, this time forcing the American Giants into oblivion. The shortstop then journeyed east and inked a deal with the Newark Eagles.

The black press dubbed the New Jersey quartet of Wells, Ray Dandridge, Mule Suttles, and Dick Seay, "The Million Dollar Infield." In the writers' opinion, that amount represented Newark's wealth if their infielders had been white.

Wells' outstanding leadership ability and intelligence led the Manleys to name him Eagles manager. The shortstop quickly proved he understood his players.

"Anytime you know your personnel, your temperaments, your attitudes, and how you get along with your teammates and things, you're ahead of the game," the infielder observed. "I don't care about how good you are. You've got to know personalities. I guess that's the reason I had so much success in my managing."

As the Eagles skipper, Willie developed many young players. Some, such as Larry Doby, Monte Irvin, and Don Newcombe, eventually broke into the major leagues.

In 1940, Wells and the Manleys disagreed over the ballclub's operations, and the manager left the states and teamed with other baseball expatriates in Mexico. The Mexicans loved the firey infielder and his scrappy style of play. They nicknamed him "El Diablo" which translates as "The Devil."

The Texan briefly returned to the United States, but the South of the Border lifestyle continued to call out to him."Players on teams in the Mexican League live just like big leaguers," Wells explained. "We have everything first class, plus the fact that the people here are much more considerate than the American baseball fan. I mean that we are heroes here and not just ballplayers."

Willie drifted back and forth between Newark and Mexico until the end of World War II. But the differences that caused the split between him and the Manleys could never be fully reconciled. In 1946, the pair parted permanently.

As America moved into the post-war era, Negro Leaguers celebrated Jackie Robinson's entry into organized baseball. But sorrow tempered their joy. Fans, both black and white, forsook their old loyalties to the Eagles and Grays and forged new ones with the Dodgers and Indians.

Wells bounced from team to team in the late 1940s, playing and managing with the New York

Black Yankees, Baltimore Elite Giants, and Indianapolis Clowns, before finishing his playing days with the Memphis Red Sox. At the ancient baseball age of 43, Willie batted a solid .328. His Negro League career average was .364.

After a brief north-of-the-border whirl in the 1950s, the man who left Texas as boy said good-bye to baseball. Old and tired, his major league dreams only a memory, Wells finally retired his uniform and spikes, moved to New York, and took a job working in a delicatessen.

In the early '70s, Wells returned to his native Austin to aid his ailing mother. He moved into the original house on Newton Street where he was born and raised. Eventually the former Negro Leaguer's health failed as well. Diabetes left him legally blind, and he died January 22, 1989 at age 83.

The National Baseball Hall of Fame and Museum induction ceremonies for Willie "The Devil" Wells occurred on August 3, 1997. Tom Lasorda, Phil Niekro, and Nellie Fox joined Wells among baseball's elite.

Wells' daughter, Stella, spoke on his behalf. She recalled the pride and talent of former Negro Leaguers, their respect for one another, and the lobbying efforts of the late "Cool Papa" Bell on behalf of her father. Her brief remarks echoed their lifetime of friendship and camaraderie. "Cool Papa Bell, we hope you and Dad are together smiling down on us," she said, "because the Diablo is in."

Bibliography

Bak, Richard. *Turkey Stearnes and the Detroit Stars.* (Detroit, MI: Wayne State University Press, 1994).

Bankes, James. *The Pittsburgh Crawfords: The Lives and Times of Black Baseball's Most Exciting Team!* (Dubuque, IL: William Brown Publishers, 1991).

Brashler, William. *Josh Gibson: A Life in the Negro Leagues.* (New York, NY: Harper and Row, 1978).

Bruce, Janet. *The Kansas City Monarchs: Champions of Black Baseball.* (Lawrence, KS: University of Kansas Press, 1985.

Chadwick, Bruce. *When the Game was Black and White: The Illustrated History of Baseball's Negro Leagues.* (New York, NY: Abbeville Press, 1992).

Chalk, Ocania. *Pioneers of Black Sports.* (New York, NY: Dodd, Mead & Company, 1975).

Clark, Dick & Lester, Larry. *The Negro Leagues Book.* (Cleveland, OH: Society for American Baseball Research, 1994).

Cooper, Michael. *Playing America's Game: The Story of Negro League Baseball.* (New York, NY: Lodestar Books, 1993).

Craft, David. *The Negro Leagues: 40 Years of Black*

Professional Baseball in Words and Pictures. (Avenel, NJ: Crescent Books, 1993).

Dixon, Phil S. & Hannigan, Patrick. *The Negro Baseball Leagues: A Photographic History, 1867-1955.* (Mattituck, NY: Amereon House, 1992).

Gardner, Robert & Shortelle, Dennis. *The Forgotten Players, The Story of Black Baseball in America.* (New York, NY: Walker and Company, 1993).

Hardwick, Leon Herbert. *Blacks in Baseball.* (Los Angeles, CA: Pilot Historical Association, 1980).

Hardwick, Leon & Manley, Effa. *Negro Baseball, Before Integration* (Chicago, IL: Adam Press, 1976).

Holway, John B. *Black Diamonds: Life in the Negro Leagues from the Men Who Lived It.* (Westport, CT: Meckler Books, 1989).
    Blackball Stars: Negro League Pioneers. (Westport, CT: Meckler Books, 1988).
    Bullet Joe and the Monarchs. (Washington, DC: Capital Press, 1984).
    Josh and Satch: The Life and Times of Josh Gibson and Satchel Paige. (Westport, CT: Meckler Books, 1991).
    The Father of Black Baseball: Rube Foster. (Washington, DC: Pretty Pages, 1981).
    Voices from the Great Black Baseball Leagues. (New York, NY: Dodd, Mead Company, 1975).

Humphrey, Kathryn Long. *Satchel Paige.* (New York, NY: Franklin Watts, 1988.

Lanctot, Neil. *Fair Dealing and Clean Playing: The Hilldale Club and the Development of Black Professional Baseball, 1910-1932.* (Jefferson, North Carolina: McFarland & Co., 1994).

Lebovitz, Hal with Satchel Paige. *Satchel Paige's Own Story: 'Pitchin' Man* (No city listed: 1948).

Margolies, Jacob. *The Negro Leagues: The Story of Black Baseball.* (Chicago, IL: Franklin Watts, 1993).

Overmyer, James. *Effa Manley and the Newark Eagles.* (Metuchen, New Jersey: Scarecrow Books, 1993).

Paige, LeRoy "Satchel" (as told to David Lipman). *Maybe I'll Pitch Forever.* (Garden City, NY: Doubleday & Company, 1961).

Peterson, Robert. *Only the Ball Was White: A History of Legendary Black Players and All-Black Professional Teams.* (Englewood Cliffs, NJ: Prentice-Hall Publishers, 1970).

Rendle, Ellen. *Judy Johnson: Delaware's Invisible Hero.* (Wilmington, DE: The Cedar Tree Press, Inc., 1995).

Ribowsky, Mark. *The Power and the Darkness: The Life of Josh Gibson in the Shadows of the Game.*(New York, NY: SImon & Schuster, 1996).

Riley, James A. *Dandy, Day and the Devil: a Trilogy of Negro League Baseball.* (Cocoa, FL: TK Publishers, 1987).
    The Biographical Encyclopedia of the Negro Baseball Leagues. (New York, NY: Carroll & Graf, 1994).
    Buck Leonard: The Black Lou Gehrig, An Autobiography. (New York, NY: Carroll & Graf, 1995).

Rogosin, Donn. *Invisible Men: Life in the Negro Leagues.* (New York, NY: G. P. Putnam's Sons, 1972).

Rubin, Robert. *Satchel Paige, All-Time Baseball Great.* (New York, NY: G. P. Putnam's Sons, 1974).

Ruck, Rob. *The Tropic of Baseball: Baseball in the*

Dominican Republic. (Westport, CT: Meckler Publishing, 1991).

Ward, Geoffrey C. and Burns, Ken with O'Connor, Jim. *Shadow Ball: The History of the Negro Leagues.* (New York: NY: Alfred A. Knopf, 1995).

White, Sol. *Sol White's History of Colored Baseball: With Other Documents of the Early BlackGame, 1886- 1936,* with introduction by Jerry Malloy. (University of Nebraska Press, 1995).

Whitehead, Charles E. *A Man and His Diamonds: The Story of Rube Foster.* (New York, NY: Vantage Press, 1980).

Young, A. S. "Doc") *Great Negro Baseball Stars and How They Made the Major Leagues.* (New York, NY; A. S. Barnes, 1953).

Index

Aaron, Henry   10, 67, 96

Alexander, Grover Cleveland   82

Allen, Dick   68

Ames, Leon "Red"   92

Bankhead, Sam   35, 56

Banks, Ernie   56, 86

Barnhill, Dave   101, 105

Benjamin, Jerry   19

Blackwell, Ewell (The Whip)   109

Blaylock, Jane   73

Boudreau, Lou   22

Brown, Willard   110

Bruton, Bill   67

Campanella, Roy   58, 106

Churchill, Neil   18

Cole, Robert   130

Comiskey, Charles   93

Crutchfield, John (Jimmie)   32

Dean, Jay Hanna (Dizzy)   17, 67

Dixon, Herbert (Rap)   112

Doby, Larry   67, 96, 131

Dougherty, Pat   93

Drew, John   65

Dykes, Jimmie   65

Easter, Luke   45

Easterling, Howard   20

Eggleston, Macajah (Mac)   112

Fielder, Benny   115

Fields, Wilmer   45

Finley, Charlie   24

Francis, Billy   83

Gans, Robert (Judy) 64, 83

Gardner, Floyd (Jelly) 94

Gatewood, Bill 52

Gibson, Josh, Jr. 33, 34, 45

Giles, George 130

Grant, Charlie 81

Greenlee, William Augustus (Gus) 16, 18, 34, 35, 55, 66, 74

Gruhler, Whitey 85

Harris, Vic 2-. 31. 35. 56

Hayward, Handy 67

Heath, Tommy 105

Heintzelman, Ken 110

Hines, Wilbur 14

Holloway, Christopher (Cruch) 52

Howard, Elston 56

Irons, Anita 63

Irvin, Monte 58, 96, 131

Johnson, Ban 97

Klieman, Ed 22

Lemon, Bob 22, 54, 76

Lewis, Cary B. 80

Lundy, Dick 103

Lyons, Jimmy 72

Mack, Connie 84, 91

Mackey, Raleigh (Biz 52, 127)

Malarcher, Dave 72, 95, 123

Manley, Abe 113

Manley, Effa 18, 113

Marquez, Luis 45

Marshall, Jack 35

Mason, Helen 33

Mathewson, Christy 92

Mays, Willie 33, 46, 96

McDermott, Mickey 105

McGinnity, John "Iron Man" 92

McGraw, John 81, 84, 92, 97

Legendary Players of the Negro Baseball Leagues

McNair, Hurley   128

Minoso, Minnie   67

Newcombe, Don   131

O'Neil, John Jordan (Buck)   20

Petway, Bruce   93

Posey, Cumberland (Cum)   32, 36, 44, 56, 74

Radcliffe, Alex   130

Riggins, Bill   128

Robinson, Jackie   9. 21. 07

Ryan, Rosy   105

Saperstein, Abe   21, 24, 123

Scales, George   84

Seay, Dick   113, 131

Stuart, Jennie   119

Suttles, George (Mule)   113, 130, 131

Taylor, Ben   43, 52

Taylor, C. I.   43, 72

Taylor, James (Candy Jim)   102, 112

Tinker, Harold   30

Trent, Ted   130

Trujillo, Rafael   18, 56, 75

Veeck, Bill   21, 23, 24, 46

Wagner, Honus   86

Walker, Harry (The Hat)   110

Webb, Norman "Tweed"   92

White, Sol   81

Wickware, Frank   93

Wilhelm, Hoyt   105

Wilkinson, J. L.   19

Williams, Bobby   83

Williams, Joseph (Smoky Joe)   31, 44, 83

Wyrostek, Johnny   110

Yancey, Bill   54

Yastrzemski, Carl   25

Zientara, Benny   110

NOV 2000